PRAYER POINTS

FOR

STUDENTS

TARGETED PRAYERS FOR DIVINE RESULTS

EDDIE JAMES

PRAYER POINTS FOR STUDENTS

PRAYER POINTS FOR STUDENTS

PNEUMA LIFE PUBLISHING

Pneuma Life Publishing books are available at discounted prices for bulk purchase for fund-raising, premiums, sales promotions.

For details, email your request to **sales@pneumalife.com** or write us at **Pneuma Life Publishing, 12138 Central Ave, Suite 251, Mitchellville, MD 20721**

Prayer Points for Students
Published by Pneuma Life Publishing
12138 Central Ave, Suite 251,
Mitchellville, MD 20721
www.pneumalife.com

First Edition: February 2024

Unless otherwise noted, all Sciptures quotations are from the KJV of the Bible

Printed in the United States of America
ISBN 978-1-56229-887-6

Table of Contents

Prayer Points for Students

Section 1
Prayers for Academic Success

Section 2
Prayers for Personal Growth

Section 3
Prayers for Healthy Relationships

Section 4 Prayers for Time Management

Section 5
Prayers for Friendships

Section 6
Prayers During Challenging Times

Section 8
Prayers for Career Discernment

INTRODUCTION

Life is a beautiful and complex tapestry. It is especially so when you are a student, stepping into the academic realm, teetering on the cusp of adulthood. This period of your life is one filled with the promise of growth, expansion of your intellectual horizons, and the blossoming of your unique abilities. However, it also brings forth trials and tribulations, moments of self-doubt, peer pressure, stress, and the anxieties of carving out your own identity in this vast world.

It is often said that we learn more about ourselves in times of adversity than in times of comfort. Students, be assured that the same holds true for you. This book, "Prayer Points for Students," is a beacon of light designed to guide you through those challenging times and celebrate with you in times of victory.

Scripture tells us in Jeremiah 29:11, "For I know the plans I have for you, declares the Lord, plans for welfare and not for evil, to give you a future and a hope." This book is a testament to that promise. It's an offering of hope, filled with divinely inspired prayers that cater to every facet of your student life. Whether it be seeking strength in the face of rigorous academic demands, managing time effectively, building self-confidence, navigating the nuances of peer dynamics, or appreciating the joy of accomplishments, you will find a prayer point for it here.

This collection of prayers is more than just a book—it is a channel through which you can communicate with God about the circumstances that shape your life as a student. It is a safe space where you can lay bare your fears, aspirations, doubts, and triumphs before the throne of God, knowing that He is ever ready to listen, guide, and provide.

As you delve into these pages, remember that each prayer is firmly rooted in the Word of God, the very bedrock of our faith. I encourage you to read and pray with an open heart and a receptive spirit, allowing the Spirit of God to work in and through you. Each prayer point is a conversation starter with God, a means to draw you closer to Him, and a tool to help you understand and apply the wisdom of His Word to your life. When we pray, we are acknowledging our need for God and inviting His divine intervention into our lives. And when we invite God into our lives, miracles happen.

As you journey through your academic life, I want you to remember this - you are not alone. The God who helped David slay Goliath, the God who was with Daniel in the lion's den, is the same God who is with you in every study session, every exam, and every decision you make.

I pray that "Prayer Points for Students" will become your spiritual companion, offering you comfort and divine wisdom during your academic journey. As you walk this path, know that you are enveloped in God's unfailing love and abiding grace. Welcome to this journey. Welcome to a conversation with God. Welcome to "Prayer Points for Students."

SECTION 1

PRAYERS FOR ACADEMIC SUCCESS

Praying For Wisdom In Understanding Complex Subjects

God, I seek Your guidance in understanding that which is difficult for me. Grant me the wisdom to grasp the complex, the patience to learn, and the humility to admit when I need help. May I always remember that, If any of you lacks wisdom, let him ask God, who gives generously to all without reproach, and it will be given him. (James 1:5)

God, I approach Your throne with a humble heart, beseeching You to enlighten my mind. Enable me to comprehend the complexities of my subject, as Your word is a lamp to my feet and a light to my path. (Psalm 119:105)

Lord, You who hold the wisdom of the ages, I implore You to help me perceive the intricate subjects before me. Guide my thinking and clear my confusion, for The unfolding of your words gives light; it imparts understanding to the simple. (Psalm 119:130)

Almighty God, I pray for Your divine insight as I navigate complex topics. May Your wisdom flow through me, so that my understanding is rooted in truth. For the Lord gives wisdom; from his mouth come knowledge and understanding. (Proverbs 2:6)

Lord Jesus, give me a discerning heart that I may gain a profound understanding of complicated subjects. Help me to Trust in the Lord with all your heart, and do not lean on your own understanding. (Proverbs 3:5)

Lord Jesus, I ask for Your wisdom in understanding these complex issues. Teach me to rely on You, to learn from You, and remember that, Take my yoke upon you, and learn from me, for I am gentle and lowly in heart, and you will find rest for your souls. (Matthew 11:29)

Praying For Wisdom In Understanding Complex Subjects

God of all wisdom, I humbly ask for Your help in my quest for understanding. Let me not be overwhelmed by the complexity but grant me peace and clarity, for You will keep in perfect peace those whose minds are steadfast, because they trust in you. (Isaiah 26:3)

Father God, I pray for Your wisdom in comprehending intricate s ubjects. Remind me that I am never alone in this journey, as the Helper, the Holy Spirit, whom the Father will send in my name, he will teach you all things and bring to your remembrance all that I have said to you. (John 14:26)

Holy Father, I come before You, seeking wisdom to unravel the complex subjects I face. Empower me to discern and understand, for I trust in Your promise that, My sheep hear my voice, and I know them, and they follow me. (John 10:27)

Dear God, as I approach the complexities of my studies, I ask for Your wisdom and understanding. You are my teacher and guide, for He teaches the humble his way. (Psalm 25:9).

Seeking Clarity And Insight During Exams And Assessments

Merciful Father, as I prepare for these assessments, grant me clear thinking and accurate recall. Help me to trust in Your provision, for Blessed is the one who trusts in the Lord, who does not look to the proud, to those who turn aside to false gods. (Psalm 40:4)

Seeking Clarity And Insight During Exams And Assessments

Loving Father, as I approach my exams, I humbly ask for clarity of mind and calmness of spirit. Guide me through each question, and may Your wisdom light my path. Remind me that, I can do all things through Christ who strengthens me. (Philippians 4:13)

God, I seek Your guidance during these assessments. Please grant me insight, and help me recall the knowledge I have studied. May I remember that, The Lord is my helper; I will not fear; what can man do to me? (Hebrews 13:6)

Lord of all wisdom, as I face these exams, please clear my mind of anxiety and fill it with understanding. Bless my efforts and let them bear fruit, for In all your ways acknowledge him, and he will make straight your paths. (Proverbs 3:6)

Almighty God, I ask for Your divine clarity during my exams. Let me understand each question clearly and recall all that I have studied. I lean on Your promise that, The Lord gives wisdom; from his mouth come knowledge and understanding. (Proverbs 2:6)

God, I pray for the insight to understand and answer my assessments effectively. Let Your peace reign in my heart, dispelling all fear and confusion, for You keep him in perfect peace whose mind is stayed on you, because he trusts in you. (Isaiah 26:3)

Lord Jesus, I approach my exams with faith, knowing You are with me. Please guide my thoughts and my pen. May I remember that, Do not be anxious about anything, but in everything by prayer and supplication with thanksgiving let your requests be made known to God. (Philippians 4:6)

Seeking Clarity And Insight During Exams And Assessments

Holy God, I humbly seek Your guidance and clarity during my exams. Remind me to rely on You in all circumstances, knowing The fear of the Lord is the beginning of wisdom; all those who practice it have a good understanding. (Psalm 111:10)

God of knowledge, as I sit for these assessments, give me clear understanding and insight. Let my hard work be fruitful, for I believe in Your words, Whatever you do, work heartily, as for the Lord and not for men. (Colossians 3:23)

Jehovah Jireh, I seek Your favor in my exams. Grant me wisdom and understanding to answer correctly and confidently. May I always remember that, But they who wait for the Lord shall renew their strength; they shall mount up with wings like eagles; they shall run and not be weary; they shall walk and not faint. (Isaiah 40:31)

Asking For Focus And Concentration During Study Sessions

God of all knowledge, as I prepare for my study session, please provide me with the concentration I need to succeed. Let Your word guide me as it says, Let the words of my mouth and the meditation of my heart be acceptable in your sight, O Lord, my rock and my redeemer. (Psalm 19:14)

Merciful Father, grant me the grace to focus and understand during my studies. Let Your peace envelope me and increase my knowledge, for Peace I leave with you; my peace I give to you. Not as the world gives do I give to you. Let not your hearts be troubled, neither let them be afraid. (John 14:27)

Asking For Focus And Concentration During Study Sessions

God, as I embark on this study session, I seek Your guidance. Grant me focus and concentration, so I may gain a deeper understanding. Remind me of Your promise that, This God—his way is perfect; the word of the Lord proves true; he is a shield for all those who take refuge in him. (Psalm 18:30)

Almighty God, I call upon Your strength as I delve into my studies. Bless me with a calm mind, free from distractions, for You will keep in perfect peace those whose minds are steadfast, because they trust in you. (Isaiah 26:3)

Loving Father, as I study, please help me to focus. Let not my mind wander, but stay rooted in the task at hand. I believe that, The steadfast love of the Lord never ceases; his mercies never come to an end; they are new every morning. (Lamentations 3:22-23)

God of wisdom, I pray for Your divine focus during my study sessions. Guide my thoughts, help me to absorb and remember. I trust in Your words that, But the Helper, the Holy Spirit, whom the Father will send in my name, he will teach you all things and bring to your remembrance all that I have said to you. (John 14:26)

Lord, You who calms the seas, still my restless mind as I study. Help me to concentrate and understand. May I always remember that, Be still, and know that I am God. I will be exalted among the nations, I will be exalted in the earth! (Psalm 46:10)

Lord Jesus, as I delve into my studies, I seek Your wisdom and focus. Clear my mind of any distractions, and help me to concentrate, for Commit your work to the Lord, and your plans will be established. (Proverbs 16:3)

Asking For Focus And Concentration During Study Sessions

Dear God, as I study, grant me the ability to concentrate and understand deeply. Bless my efforts and let them bear fruit, for In all your ways acknowledge him, and he will make straight your paths. (Proverbs 3:6)

Lord of Heaven, as I commit myself to this session of study, I pray for focus and a clear mind. Enable me to discern and comprehend, for Your word is a lamp to my feet and a light to my path. (Psalm 119:105)

Creativity And Innovation In Problem-Solving

God of all knowledge, I ask for Your creative spirit as I confront these problems. Enlighten me with fresh perspectives and inventive solutions, for Your word is a lamp to my feet and a light to my path. (Psalm 119:105)

Lord, I invoke Your wisdom as I address these challenges. Spark my creativity and guide me to new, innovative solutions, for It is the glory of God to conceal things, but the glory of kings is to search things out. (Proverbs 25:2)

God, as I seek to solve these problems, I ask for Your divine creativity. Illuminate my mind with innovative ideas, for In your light we see light. (Psalm 36:9)

God, the ultimate Creator, bless my efforts to find solutions to these problems. Inspire me with creativity and innovation, for The earth is the Lord's, and everything in it, the world, and all who live in it. (Psalm 24:1)

CREATIVITY AND INNOVATION IN PROBLEM-SOLVING

God, as I tackle these challenges, I ask for Your divine inspiration. May my thoughts be guided by Your wisdom, enabling me to devise creative solutions. I remember Your words, Call to me and I will answer you, and will tell you great and hidden things that you have not known. (Jeremiah 33:3)

Almighty God, I seek Your wisdom in problem-solving. Grant me creativity and innovation to develop new solutions, for See, I am doing a new thing! Now it springs up; do you not perceive it? I am making a way in the wilderness and streams in the wasteland. (Isaiah 43:19)

Lord Jesus, I ask for Your guidance as I work through these problems. Enlighten my mind, spark my creativity, and help me innovate, as it is written, I can do all things through Christ who strengthens me. (Philippians 4:13)

God of wisdom, as I face these issues, I pray for Your divine inspiration. Infuse me with creativity and inventiveness to devise effective solutions, for The Lord gives wisdom; from his mouth come knowledge and understanding. (Proverbs 2:6)

Merciful Father, I ask for Your help in problem-solving. Let my mind be open to new ideas, and guide me to innovative solutions, for Trust in the Lord with all your heart, and do not lean on your own understanding. In all your ways acknowledge him, and he will make straight your paths. (Proverbs 3:5-6)

God, as I approach these challenges, I pray for Your guidance. Inspire me to think creatively and come up with innovative solutions, for My thoughts are nothing like your thoughts, says the Lord. And my ways are far beyond anything you could imagine. (Isaiah 55:8)

Creativity And Innovation In Problem-Solving

God of all knowledge, I ask for Your creative spirit as I confront these problems. Enlighten me with fresh perspectives and inventive solutions, for Your word is a lamp to my feet and a light to my path. (Psalm 119:105)

Lord, I invoke Your wisdom as I address these challenges. Spark my creativity and guide me to new, innovative solutions, for It is the glory of God to conceal things, but the glory of kings is to search things out. (Proverbs 25:2)

God, as I seek to solve these problems, I ask for Your divine creativity. Illuminate my mind with innovative ideas, for In your light we see light. (Psalm 36:9)

God, the ultimate Creator, bless my efforts to find solutions to these problems. Inspire me with creativity and innovation, for The earth is the Lord's, and everything in it, the world, and all who live in it. (Psalm 24:1)

Requesting Guidance In Choosing The Right Course Or Major

Loving Lord, as I contemplate my course, I pray for Your divine direction. Lead me to a path that fulfills my purpose and serves Your kingdom, for Each of you should use whatever gift you have received to serve others, as faithful stewards of God's grace in its various forms. (1 Peter 4:10)

REQUESTING GUIDANCE IN CHOOSING THE RIGHT COURSE OR MAJOR

God, as I stand at the crossroads of choosing my course, I seek Your divine guidance. May Your wisdom illuminate the right path for me, for Your word is a lamp to my feet and a light to my path.
(Psalm 119:105)

Lord, I stand before You, seeking Your wisdom in choosing my major. I place my future in Your hands, trusting that, For I know the plans I have for you, declares the Lord, plans for welfare and not for evil, to give you a future and a hope. (Jeremiah 29:11)

Almighty God, as I contemplate my course of study, guide me to choose what aligns with Your will for me. May my decision be rooted in Your words that, In all your ways acknowledge him, and he will make straight your paths. (Proverbs 3:6)

God, as I seek to choose the right major, I pray for Your wisdom and direction. Help me discern the path that aligns with my talents and Your plans, for The heart of man plans his way, but the Lord establishes his steps. (Proverbs 16:9)

Lord Jesus, I ask for Your guidance in selecting my course. Illuminate my mind and guide my heart towards the path You've designed for me, for Jesus answered, 'I am the way and the truth and the life. No one comes to the Father except through me.' (John 14:6)

God of wisdom, as I stand at the threshold of a significant decision, grant me clarity in choosing the right major. May I always remember that, Trust in the Lord with all your heart, and do not lean on your own understanding. (Proverbs 3:5)

Requesting Guidance In Choosing The Right Course Or Major

God, I seek Your wisdom in choosing my major. Guide me to a field where I can both grow and serve, for Therefore, as we have opportunity, let us do good to all people, especially to those who belong to the family of believers. (Galatians 6:10)

Merciful God, as I decide on my course, I ask for Your insight and direction. Help me to discern my calling and to follow Your will, for I can do all this through him who gives me strength. (Philippians 4:13)

Dear God, as I stand on the precipice of this decision, I ask for Your divine guidance in choosing the right major. Direct my steps according to Your love and wisdom, for The Lord will guide you continually, giving you plenty of water when you are dry and restoring your strength. You will be like a well-watered garden, like an ever-flowing spring. (Isaiah 58:11)

Praying For Success In Research Projects And Presentations

Merciful God, bless my efforts in this research project. Help me to uncover truths and contribute valuable insights, for The Lord gives wisdom; from his mouth come knowledge and understanding. (Proverbs 2:6)

Lord of Heaven, as I stand to present, grant me Your peace and clarity. Let my words be well received and effective, for Therefore, having this ministry by the mercy of God, we do not lose heart. (2 Corinthians 4:1)

Praying For Success In Research Projects And Presentations

God, as I embark on this research project, I seek Your guidance. May Your wisdom be with me at every step, aiding my success, as You have promised, Commit your work to the Lord, and your plans will be established. (Proverbs 16:3)

God, as I prepare for this presentation, I ask for Your divine inspiration. Allow my words to flow clearly and my points to resonate, for The heart of the wise makes his speech judicious and adds persuasiveness to his lips. (Proverbs 16:23)

Almighty Lord, I seek Your wisdom and clarity for my research project. Let every effort I put into this work yield fruitful results, for Whatever you do, work heartily, as for the Lord and not for men. (Colossians 3:23)

God of all knowledge, I approach this presentation with humility, asking for Your guidance. Let my words be clear and my message compelling, for A word fitly spoken is like apples of gold in a setting of silver. (Proverbs 25:11)

Dear Father, as I embark on this research, I seek Your divine guidance. Grant me understanding and discernment, ensuring my success, as In all your ways acknowledge him, and he will make straight your paths. (Proverbs 3:6)

Loving Lord, as I prepare for my presentation, let Your wisdom guide me. Help me to communicate effectively and confidently, for Let your speech always be gracious, seasoned with salt, so that you may know how you ought to answer each person. (Colossians 4:6)

Praying For Success In Research Projects And Presentations

Almighty God, guide me in my research endeavors. Lead me to valuable insights and successful conclusions, for I can do all things through Christ who strengthens me. (Philippians 4:13)

Dear God, as I prepare my presentation, may I communicate effectively and confidently. Grant me success, for For God has not given us a spirit of fear, but of power and of love and of a sound mind. (2 Timothy 1:7)

Seeking Divine Help In Understanding Challenging Concepts

Loving God, I ask for Your help in understanding these complex topics. Open my mind and heart to receive Your divine wisdom, for And we know that the Son of God has come and has given us understanding, so that we may know him who is true; and we are in him who is true, in his Son Jesus Christ. (1 John 5:20)

Merciful God, as I struggle with these challenging concepts, I seek Your wisdom. Enlighten my mind and guide my understanding, for For the Lord gives wisdom; from his mouth come knowledge and understanding. (Proverbs 2:6)

Mighty God, as I strive to comprehend these complex ideas, I pray for Your divine insight. Expand my understanding and guide my thoughts, for Trust in the Lord with all your heart, and do not lean on your own understanding. (Proverbs 3:5)

Seeking Divine Help In Understanding Challenging Concepts

God, as I delve into these challenging concepts, I seek Your wisdom and guidance. Help me comprehend and master them, for Your word is a lamp to my feet and a light to my path. (Psalm 119:105)

Almighty God, I seek Your divine aid as I confront these complex ideas. Open my mind and deepen my understanding, for The Lord gives wisdom; from his mouth come knowledge and understanding. (Proverbs 2:6)

Lord Jesus, I pray for Your divine intervention in understanding these difficult concepts. Guide my mind and heart to comprehend them, for If any of you lacks wisdom, let him ask God, who gives generously to all without reproach, and it will be given him. (James 1:5)

Lord Jesus, I pray for Your guidance in tackling these challenging ideas. Enlighten me and expand my comprehension, for I am the light of the world. Whoever follows me will not walk in darkness, but will have the light of life. (John 8:12)

God, I ask for Your divine wisdom as I explore these complex subjects. May Your spirit enlighten my understanding, for But the Helper, the Holy Spirit, whom the Father will send in my name, he will teach you all things and bring to your remembrance all that I have said to you. (John 14:26)

God of all knowledge, I seek Your guidance in grasping these challenging concepts. Grant me discernment and understanding, for In all your ways acknowledge him, and he will make straight your paths. (Proverbs 3:6)

Seeking Divine Help In Understanding Challenging Concepts

Lord Jesus, I pray for Your divine wisdom as I delve into these challenging subjects. Help me grasp and master them, for Blessed are those who find wisdom, those who gain understanding. (Proverbs 3:13)

Asking for effective time management for academic tasks

Mighty God, I pray for Your wisdom and guidance in managing my time. Grant me the ability to efficiently handle my academic tasks, for But seek first the kingdom of God and his righteousness, and all these things will be added to you. (Matthew 6:33)

God of all wisdom, I ask for Your divine help in managing my time. Teach me to prioritize and balance my tasks effectively, for But the wisdom from above is first pure, then peaceable, gentle, open to reason, full of mercy and good fruits, impartial and sincere. (James 3:17)

Lord Jesus, as I navigate my academic duties, I pray for Your guidance in effective time management. Let every moment be utilized wisely, for The heart of man plans his way, but the Lord establishes his steps. (Proverbs 16:9)

Lord Jesus, as I seek to manage my time wisely for academic pursuits, I ask for Your guidance. Show me how to balance and prioritize effectively, for In all your ways acknowledge him, and he will make straight your paths. (Proverbs 3:6)

Asking for Effective Time Management for Academic Tasks

God, as I navigate my academic tasks, I seek Your guidance in managing my time wisely. Help me balance and prioritize, for There is a time for everything, and a season for every activity under the heavens. (Ecclesiastes 3:1)

Lord Jesus, I ask for Your wisdom in managing my time for academic pursuits. Provide me with the discipline and focus I need, for Look carefully then how you walk, not as unwise but as wise, making the best use of the time. (Ephesians 5:15-16)

God, I seek Your guidance to effectively manage my time. May I use each moment wisely to complete my academic tasks, for So teach us to number our days that we may get a heart of wisdom. (Psalm 90:12)

Almighty God, I pray for Your wisdom in managing my time. Help me to prioritize and utilize each moment effectively, for Whatever you do, work heartily, as for the Lord and not for men. (Colossians 3:23)

Loving God, I ask for Your guidance in managing my academic tasks efficiently. May I honor You with my time and effort, for The plans of the diligent lead surely to abundance, but everyone who is hasty comes only to poverty. (Proverbs 21:5)

Merciful Father, I seek Your wisdom in managing my time effectively. Let my efforts bear fruit, for Commit your work to the Lord, and your plans will be established. (Proverbs 16:3)

Perseverance and Resilience in the Face of Academic Challenges

God, as I face these academic challenges, I pray for Your strength and perseverance. Guide me, for I can do all things through Christ who strengthens me. (Philippians 4:13)

Gracious Lord, I seek Your divine resilience as I confront these academic hurdles. Uphold me, for Blessed is the one who perseveres under trial because, having stood the test, that person will receive the crown of life that the Lord has promised to those who love him. (James 1:12)

Almighty God, as I navigate these academic challenges, I pray for perseverance. Inspire me to endure and overcome, for Let us not become weary in doing good, for at the proper time we will reap a harvest if we do not give up. (Galatians 6:9)

Lord Jesus, in the face of these academic difficulties, I seek Your strength and resilience. Carry me through, for The Lord is my strength and my shield; my heart trusts in him, and he helps me. (Psalm 28:7)

God of all wisdom, I pray for perseverance as I face these academic trials. Guide my steps and strengthen me, for But those who hope in the LORD will renew their strength. They will soar on wings like eagles; they will run and not grow weary, they will walk and not be faint. (Isaiah 40:31)

Loving Father, I seek Your divine strength and resilience in these academic challenges. Strengthen my spirit, for Be strong and courageous. Do not be afraid or terrified because of them, for the LORD your God goes with you; he will never leave you nor forsake you. (Deuteronomy 31:6)

Perseverance and Resilience in the Face of Academic Challenges

Merciful God, I ask for Your divine perseverance as I face these academic trials. Uphold me and guide me, for My flesh and my heart may fail, but God is the strength of my heart and my portion forever. (Psalm 73:26)

Lord Jesus, I pray for Your strength and resilience as I navigate these academic difficulties. Give me perseverance to endure, for In the world you will have tribulation. But take heart; I have overcome the world. (John 16:33)

God, I seek Your guidance and strength to persevere in my academic journey. May Your resilience flow through me, for And let us not grow weary of doing good, for in due season we will reap, if we do not give up. (Galatians 6:9)

Lord Jesus, as I face these academic challenges, I ask for Your divine strength and perseverance. Guide me, for But he said to me, 'My grace is sufficient for you, for my power is made perfect in weakness.' Therefore I will boast all the more gladly about my weaknesses, so that Christ's power may rest on me. (2 Corinthians 12:9)

Praying for the Ability to Retain and Recall Information Effectively

Lord Jesus, I pray for Your divine help to retain and recall this knowledge. Strengthen my memory, for My son, do not forget my teaching, but keep my commands in your heart. (Proverbs 3:1)

PRAYING FOR THE ABILITY TO RETAIN AND RECALL INFORMATION EFFECTIVELY

God, as I seek to retain and recall this information, I ask for Your divine help. Strengthen my memory, for The Helper, the Holy Spirit, will teach you all things and bring to your remembrance all that I have said to you. (John 14:26)

Gracious Lord, I pray for the ability to remember and retrieve this knowledge effectively. Guide my mind, for For the Lord gives wisdom; from his mouth come knowledge and understanding. (Proverbs 2:6)

Almighty God, as I study, I pray for Your assistance in retaining this information. Help me recall it when needed, for But the Counselor, the Holy Spirit, whom the Father will send in my name, will teach you all things and will remind you of everything I have said to you. (John 14:26)

Lord Jesus, I seek Your divine aid in retaining and recalling this knowledge. Grant me a sharp memory, for But the wisdom from above is first pure, then peaceable, gentle, open to reason, full of mercy and good fruits, impartial and sincere. (James 3:17)

God of all wisdom, I pray for Your help in remembering this information. Strengthen my mind, for In all your ways acknowledge him, and he will make straight your paths. (Proverbs 3:6)

Loving Father, I ask for Your assistance in retaining this knowledge. Help me recall it accurately, for Trust in the LORD with all your heart and lean not on your own understanding. (Proverbs 3:5)

Merciful God, as I study, I seek Your help in retaining this information. Guide my memory, for I can do all things through him who strengthens me. (Philippians 4:13)

Praying for the Ability to Retain and Recall Information Effectively

God, I seek Your guidance in retaining this information. Grant me the ability to recall it effectively, for He gives power to the faint, and to him who has no might he increases strength. (Isaiah 40:29)

Lord Jesus, as I endeavor to retain this knowledge, I ask for Your divine help. Guide my memory, for Call to me and I will answer you, and will tell you great and hidden things that you have not known. (Jeremiah 33:3)

Seeking Confidence And Self-Belief In Academic Pursuits

Merciful God, as I continue my academic journey, I pray for Your guidance to foster self-belief. Let me embrace the strength You've given me, for Fear not, for I am with you; be not dismayed, for I am your God; I will strengthen you, I will help you, I will uphold you with my righteous right hand. (Isaiah 41:10)

Lord Jesus, I seek Your wisdom to inspire self-confidence within me. As I strive to excel in my studies, remind me of my capabilities, for In all your ways acknowledge him, and he will make straight your paths. (Proverbs 3:6)

God, I pray for Your divine intervention to instill self-belief. Remind me of the strength within me as I pursue my academic goals, for The LORD is my light and my salvation; whom shall I fear? The LORD is the stronghold of my life; of whom shall I be afraid? (Psalm 27:1)

Seeking Confidence And Self-Belief In Academic Pursuits

God, as I pursue my studies, I seek Your guidance to foster self-belief and confidence. Strengthen me, for I can do all things through Christ who strengthens me. (Philippians 4:13)

Gracious Lord, I pray for Your divine inspiration to instill in me self-confidence. Encourage my heart as I tread this academic path, for For God gave us a spirit not of fear but of power and love and self-control. (2 Timothy 1:7)

Almighty God, as I endeavor in my academic journey, I ask for Your aid in fostering self-belief. Empower me, for But those who hope in the LORD will renew their strength. They will soar on wings like eagles; they will run and not grow weary, they will walk and not be faint. (Isaiah 40:31)

Lord Jesus, I seek Your divine assurance to instill confidence and self-belief in me. Encourage me to pursue my academic goals, for Have I not commanded you? Be strong and courageous. Do not be afraid; do not be discouraged, for the LORD your God will be with you wherever you go. (Joshua 1:9)

God of all wisdom, I pray for Your guidance to inspire confidence within me. As I strive for academic excellence, remind me of my worth, for So God created man in his own image, in the image of God he created him; male and female he created them. (Genesis 1:27)

Loving Father, I ask for Your divine hand to guide me in building my self-confidence. Remind me that I am capable, for Trust in the LORD with all your heart and lean not on your own understanding. (Proverbs 3:5)

Seeking Confidence And Self-Belief In Academic Pursuits

Lord Jesus, as I embark on this academic journey, I seek Your guidance to foster confidence. Reaffirm in me the belief that I can overcome any hurdle, for I have said these things to you, that in me you may have peace. In the world you will have tribulation. But take heart; I have overcome the world. (John 16:33)

Praying For Resilience In The Face Of Criticism Or Failure

Merciful God, I ask for Your divine resilience as I face criticism and failure. Uphold me and guide me, for My flesh and my heart may fail, but God is the strength of my heart and my portion forever. (Psalm 73:26)

Lord Jesus, I pray for Your strength and resilience as I navigate criticism and failure. Give me the perseverance to endure, for In the world you will have tribulation. But take heart; I have overcome the world. (John 16:33)

God, I seek Your guidance and strength to persevere through criticism and failure. May Your resilience flow through me, for And let us not grow weary of doing good, for in due season we will reap, if we do not give up. (Galatians 6:9)

Lord Jesus, as I face criticism and failure, I ask for Your divine strength and perseverance. Guide me, for But he said to me, 'My grace is sufficient for you, for my power is made perfect in weakness.' Therefore I will boast all the more gladly about my weaknesses, so that Christ's power may rest on me. (2 Corinthians 12:9)

Praying For Resilience In The Face Of Criticism Or Failure

God, as I face criticism and failure, I pray for Your divine resilience. Strengthen me, for I can do all things through Christ who strengthens me. (Philippians 4:13)

Gracious Lord, I seek Your divine strength as I confront criticism and failure. Uphold me, for Blessed is the one who perseveres under trial because, having stood the test, that person will receive the crown of life that the Lord has promised to those who love him. (James 1:12)

Almighty God, as I navigate through criticism and failure, I pray for resilience. Inspire me to endure and overcome, for We are afflicted in every way, but not crushed; perplexed, but not driven to despair; persecuted, but not forsaken; struck down, but not destroyed. (2 Corinthians 4:8-9)

Lord Jesus, in the face of criticism and failure, I seek Your strength and resilience. Carry me through, for The Lord is my strength and my shield; my heart trusts in him, and he helps me. (Psalm 28:7)

God of all wisdom, I pray for resilience as I face criticism and failure. Guide my steps and strengthen me, for But those who hope in the LORD will renew their strength. They will soar on wings like eagles; they will run and not grow weary, they will walk and not be faint. (Isaiah 40:31)

Loving Father, I seek Your divine strength in facing criticism and failure. Strengthen my spirit, for Be strong and courageous. Do not be afraid or terrified because of them, for the LORD your God goes with you; he will never leave you nor forsake you. (Deuteronomy 31:6)

SECTION 2

PRAYERS FOR PERSONAL GROWTH

Asking For Emotional Stability During Stressful Periods

God, as I navigate through this stressful period, I seek Your peace for emotional stability. Comfort me, for Peace I leave with you; my peace I give to you. Not as the world gives do I give to you. Let not your hearts be troubled, neither let them be afraid. (John 14:27)

Gracious Lord, I ask for Your divine calm to bring stability to my emotions during these challenging times. Hold me, for Cast your burden on the LORD, and he will sustain you; he will never permit the righteous to be moved. (Psalm 55:22)

Almighty God, as I face stress and uncertainty, I pray for Your comfort to stabilize my emotions. Uphold me, for Come to me, all who labor and are heavy laden, and I will give you rest. (Matthew 11:28)

Lord Jesus, in this time of stress, I seek Your divine calmness. Fill me with Your peace, for Do not be anxious about anything, but in everything by prayer and supplication with thanksgiving let your requests be made known to God. (Philippians 4:6)

God of all comfort, I pray for emotional stability as I navigate this stressful time. Bring peace to my heart, for You keep him in perfect peace whose mind is stayed on you, because he trusts in you. (Isaiah 26:3)

Loving Father, I seek Your comfort and peace in this challenging period. Stabilize my emotions, for When anxiety was great within me, your consolation brought joy to my soul. (Psalm 94:19)

Merciful God, as I face stress and uncertainty, I pray for Your divine calm. Provide me emotional stability, for I have said these things to you, that in me you may have peace. In the world you will have tribulation. But take heart; I have overcome the world. (John 16:33)

Asking For Emotional Stability During Stressful Periods

Merciful God, as I face stress and uncertainty, I pray for Your divine calm. Provide me emotional stability, for I have said these things to you, that in me you may have peace. In the world you will have tribulation. But take heart; I have overcome the world. (John 16:33)

Lord Jesus, I seek Your divine peace to calm my emotions during this stressful time. Uphold me, for Casting all your anxieties on him, because he cares for you. (1 Peter 5:7)

God, I pray for Your comfort and peace as I face these challenges. Grant me emotional stability, for For God is not a God of confusion but of peace. (1 Corinthians 14:33)

Lord Jesus, during this time of stress, I seek Your divine calm. Steady my emotions, for Therefore do not worry about tomorrow, for tomorrow will worry about itself. Each day has enough trouble of its own. (Matthew 6:34)

Peace And Calmness During Exam Periods

Lord Jesus, I pray for Your peace as I face this exam. Calm my nerves, for I have said these things to you, that in me you may have peace. In the world you will have tribulation. But take heart; I have overcome the world. (John 16:33)

God, I seek Your peace and calm as I prepare for this exam. Quiet my anxieties, for The Lord gives strength to his people; the Lord blesses his people with peace. (Psalm 29:11)

Peace And Calmness During Exam Periods

God, as I enter this exam period, I seek Your peace to calm my nerves. Comfort me, for Peace I leave with you; my peace I give to you. Not as the world gives do I give to you. Let not your hearts be troubled, neither let them be afraid. (John 14:27)

Gracious Lord, during this time of testing, I pray for Your divine calm to wash over me. Still my anxieties, for Do not be anxious about anything, but in every situation, by prayer and petition, with thanksgiving, present your requests to God. (Philippians 4:6)

Almighty God, as I face this exam, I ask for Your divine peace to quiet my mind. Hold me steady, for You keep him in perfect peace whose mind is stayed on you, because he trusts in you. (Isaiah 26:3)

Lord Jesus, I seek Your tranquility as I approach this exam period. Calm my spirit, for Come to me, all you who are weary and burdened, and I will give you rest. (Matthew 11:28)

God of all wisdom, I pray for Your peace during these exams. Help me to focus and remain calm, for Be still, and know that I am God. I will be exalted among the nations, I will be exalted in the earth! (Psalm 46:10)

Loving Father, I ask for Your divine calm to permeate my being during this exam. Keep my heart steady, for Cast all your anxiety on him because he cares for you. (1 Peter 5:7)

Merciful God, in this time of testing, I seek Your peace. Soothe my worries, for The Lord is near. Do not be anxious about anything. (Philippians 4:5-6)

Peace And Calmness During Exam Periods

Lord Jesus, as I face this exam period, I ask for Your divine calmness. Settle my mind, for Therefore do not worry about tomorrow, for tomorrow will worry about itself. Each day has enough trouble of its own. (Matthew 6:34)

Requesting Courage To Speak Up And Share Opinions In Class

Lord Jesus, I pray for the courage to share my ideas in class. Embolden me, for So we can confidently say, 'The Lord is my helper; I will not fear; what can man do to me?' (Hebrews 13:6)

God, I seek Your courage to express my thoughts openly. Let my speech be gracious, for Gracious words are like a honeycomb, sweetness to the soul and health to the body. (Proverbs 16:24)

Lord Jesus, as I interact in class, I ask for Your divine courage to share my opinions. Guide my words, for But when they hand you over, do not worry about how or what you are to say; for it will be given you in that hour what you are to say. (Matthew 10:19)

Loving Father, I ask for Your divine courage to speak up in class. Inspire my words, for Let the words of my mouth and the meditation of my heart be acceptable in your sight, O LORD, my rock and my redeemer. (Psalm 19:14)

Merciful God, grant me the courage to voice my thoughts and opinions. Let my words reflect Your wisdom, for A word fitly spoken is like apples of gold in a setting of silver. (Proverbs 25:11)

Requesting Courage To Speak Up And Share Opinions In Class

God, as I navigate the classroom environment, grant me the courage to voice my thoughts. Strengthen me, for Be strong and courageous. Do not be afraid; do not be discouraged, for the LORD your God will be with you wherever you go. (Joshua 1:9)

Gracious Lord, I pray for Your divine courage to speak up in class. Guide my words, for In the same way, let your light shine before others, so that they may see your good works and give glory to your Father who is in heaven. (Matthew 5:16)

Almighty God, grant me the courage to share my opinions. Give me boldness, for The wicked flee when no one pursues, but the righteous are bold as a lion. (Proverbs 28:1)

Lord Jesus, I seek Your strength and courage to voice my thoughts in class. Empower me, for For God gave us a spirit not of fear but of power and love and self-control. (2 Timothy 1:7)

God of all wisdom, I pray for the courage to share my perspectives. May my words be beneficial, for Let no corrupting talk come out of your mouths, but only such as is good for building up, as fits the occasion, that it may give grace to those who hear. (Ephesians 4:29)

Praying For Healthy Self-Esteem And A Positive Self-Image

God, as I learn to see myself through Your eyes, I pray for healthy self-esteem and a positive self-image. Remind me, for I am fearfully and wonderfully made. Wonderful are your works; my soul knows it very well. (Psalm 139:14)

Gracious Lord, I seek Your guidance in cultivating a positive self-image. Let me remember, for But by the grace of God I am what I am, and his grace to me was not without effect. (1 Corinthians 15:10)

Almighty God, help me to appreciate the person You've made me to be. Strengthen my self-esteem, for For we are God's masterpiece. He has created us anew in Christ Jesus, so we can do the good things he planned for us long ago. (Ephesians 2:10)

Lord Jesus, guide me towards a healthy self-esteem and a positive self-image. Assure me, for So God created mankind in his own image, in the image of God he created them; male and female he created them. (Genesis 1:27)

God of all creation, I pray for a positive self-image, rooted in Your love. Validate me, for See what great love the Father has lavished on us, that we should be called children of God! (1 John 3:1)

Loving Father, I ask for Your guidance in building a healthy self-esteem. Let me recognize, for Yet you, LORD, are our Father. We are the clay, you are the potter; we are all the work of your hand. (Isaiah 64:8)

Merciful God, let me see my worth in You and develop a healthy self-image. Confirm in me, for For you formed my inward parts; you knitted me together in my mother's womb. (Psalm 139:13)

Praying For Healthy Self-Esteem And A Positive Self-Image

Lord Jesus, I pray for a positive self-image rooted in Your love. Teach me, for But the Lord said to Samuel, 'Do not consider his appearance or his height, for I have rejected him. The Lord does not look at the things people look at. People look at the outward appearance, but the Lord looks at the heart.' (1 Samuel 16:7)

God, guide me towards healthy self-esteem. Remind me, for Therefore, if anyone is in Christ, he is a new creation. The old has passed away; behold, the new has come. (2 Corinthians 5:17)

Lord Jesus, as I navigate the world, I ask for a positive self-image \rooted in Your love. Reassure me, for You have been set apart as holy to the LORD your God, and He has chosen you from all the nations of the earth to be His own special treasure. (Deuteronomy 14:2)

Seeking Guidance In Overcoming Feelings Of Inadequacy

Lord Jesus, I pray for Your guidance as I confront feelings of inadequacy. Encourage me, for Cast all your anxiety on him because he cares for you. (1 Peter 5:7)

God, I seek Your strength to overcome feelings of inadequacy. Remind me, for Being confident of this, that he who began a good work in you will carry it on to completion until the day of Christ Jesus. (Philippians 1:6)

Lord Jesus, as I navigate through feelings of inadequacy, I ask for Your divine guidance. Comfort me, for But those who hope in the LORD will renew their strength. They will soar on wings like eagles; they will run and not grow weary, they will walk and not be faint. (Isaiah 40:31)

Seeking Guidance In Overcoming Feelings Of Inadequacy

God, as I grapple with feelings of inadequacy, I seek Your guidance to overcome them. Remind me, for My grace is sufficient for you, for my power is made perfect in weakness. (2 Corinthians 12:9)

Gracious Lord, help me to trust in Your strength when I feel inadequate. Strengthen me, for I can do all things through Christ who strengthens me. (Philippians 4:13)

Almighty God, I pray for Your divine guidance in overcoming feelings of inadequacy. Guide me, for Trust in the LORD with all your heart, and do not lean on your own understanding. (Proverbs 3:5)

Lord Jesus, I seek Your help in navigating these feelings of inadequacy. Encourage me, for For I know the plans I have for you, declares the LORD, plans for welfare and not for evil, to give you a future and a hope. (Jeremiah 29:11)

God of all comfort, as I face feelings of inadequacy, I ask for Your guidance to overcome them. Remind me, for Do not fear, for I am with you; Do not anxiously look about you, for I am your God. I will strengthen you, surely I will help you, Surely I will uphold you with My righteous right hand. (Isaiah 41:10)

Loving Father, help me to trust in Your plan when I feel inadequate. Empower me, for God has not given us a spirit of fear and timidity, but of power, love, and self-discipline. (2 Timothy 1:7)

Merciful God, grant me the strength to overcome feelings of inadequacy. Inspire me, for For we are his workmanship, created in Christ Jesus for good works, which God prepared beforehand, that we should walk in them. (Ephesians 2:10)

Asking For Emotional Support During Periods Of Homesickness

God, as I navigate this period of homesickness, I seek Your comfort. Draw near to me, for Blessed are those who mourn, for they shall be comforted. (Matthew 5:4)

Gracious Lord, in this time of longing for home, I pray for Your tender care. Comfort my heart, for He heals the brokenhearted and binds up their wounds. (Psalm 147:3)

Almighty God, as I experience homesickness, I ask for Your soothing presence. Be my refuge, for God is our refuge and strength, a very present help in trouble. (Psalm 46:1)

Lord Jesus, as I miss my home, I seek Your comfort and guidance. Strengthen me, for So do not fear, for I am with you; do not be dismayed, for I am your God. I will strengthen you and help you. (Isaiah 41:10)

God of all comfort, during this period of homesickness, I pray for Your consoling presence. Hold me close, for He will cover you with his pinions, and under his wings you will find refuge. (Psalm 91:4)

Loving Father, I seek Your comfort as I navigate this homesickness. Encourage me, for Come to me, all you who are weary and burdened, and I will give you rest. (Matthew 11:28)

Merciful God, in this time of longing for home, I pray for Your tender care. Comfort my spirit, for The Lord is near to the brokenhearted and saves the crushed in spirit. (Psalm 34:18)

Lord Jesus, as I miss my home, I ask for Your comforting presence. Guide me, for I will not leave you as orphans; I will come to you. (John 14:18)

Asking For Emotional Support During Periods Of Homesickness

God, during this period of homesickness, I seek Your comforting presence. Strengthen me, for Cast your cares on the LORD and he will sustain you; he will never let the righteous be shaken. (Psalm 55:22)

Lord Jesus, as I navigate this homesickness, I pray for Your emotional support. Comfort me, for As a mother comforts her child, so will I comfort you; and you will be comforted. (Isaiah 66:13)

Joy And Enthusiasm In Learning New Things

Lord Jesus, as I engage with new knowledge, fill me with Your joy. Kindle my enthusiasm, for Instruct a wise man and he will be wiser still; teach a righteous man and he will add to his learning. (Proverbs 9:9)

God, in my journey of learning, I seek Your joy and passion. Ignite my interest, for I have more insight than all my teachers, for I meditate on your statutes. (Psalm 119:99)

Lord Jesus, I pray for Your joy and enthusiasm as I learn new things. Enlighten me, for Your word is a lamp to my feet and a light to my path. (Psalm 119:105)

Merciful God, in my quest for learning, I pray for Your joy and excitement. Brighten my spirit, for Blessed is the one who finds wisdom, and the one who gets understanding. (Proverbs 3:13)

Joy And Enthusiasm In Learning New Things

God, as I embark on new learning experiences, I ask for Your joy and enthusiasm to guide me. Ignite my spirit, for The precepts of the Lord are right, rejoicing the heart; the commandment of the Lord is pure, enlightening the eyes. (Psalm 19:8)

Gracious Lord, I seek Your inspiration as I learn new things. Fill me with joy, for Your words were found, and I ate them, and your words became to me a joy and the delight of my heart. (Jeremiah 15:16)

Almighty God, I ask for Your joy and excitement as I delve into new knowledge. Awaken my curiosity, for If any of you lacks wisdom, let him ask God, who gives generously to all without reproach, and it will be given him. (James 1:5)

Lord Jesus, I pray for enthusiasm and joy in my pursuit of learning. Invigorate my spirit, for For the Lord gives wisdom; from his mouth come knowledge and understanding. (Proverbs 2:6)

God of all wisdom, as I learn new things, fill me with joy and passion. Enliven my understanding, for An intelligent heart acquires knowledge, and the ear of the wise seeks knowledge. (Proverbs 18:15)

Loving Father, I seek Your joy as I explore new areas of knowledge. Fuel my enthusiasm, for The heart of the discerning acquires knowledge, for the ears of the wise seek it out. (Proverbs 18:15)

Praying For The Ability To Manage Stress And Anxiety Effectively

God, as I face stress and anxiety, I ask for Your calming presence. Strengthen me, for Do not be anxious about anything, but in every situation, by prayer and petition, with thanksgiving, present your requests to God. (Philippians 4:6)

Gracious Lord, I seek Your peace as I navigate stress. Bring tranquility to my heart, for Peace I leave with you; my peace I give to you. Not as the world gives do I give to you. Let not your hearts be troubled, neither let them be afraid. (John 14:27)

Almighty God, I ask for Your grace in managing anxiety and stress. Reassure me, for Cast all your anxiety on him because he cares for you. (1 Peter 5:7)

Lord Jesus, I pray for Your guidance in handling stress effectively. Remind me, for Fear not, for I am with you; Be not dismayed, for I am your God. I will strengthen you, Yes, I will help you, I will uphold you with My righteous right hand. (Isaiah 41:10)

God of all comfort, in moments of stress, I seek Your calming presence. Comfort me, for The LORD is near to all who call on him, to all who call on him in truth. (Psalm 145:18)

Loving Father, I pray for Your strength in managing anxiety. Uphold me, for I can do all things through him who strengthens me. (Philippians 4:13)

Merciful God, I ask for Your guidance in handling stress. Reassure me, for For God has not given us a spirit of fear, but of power and of love and of a sound mind. (2 Timothy 1:7)

Praying For The Ability To Manage Stress And Anxiety Effectively

Lord Jesus, as I navigate stress, I ask for Your peace. Calm my spirit, for Come to me, all who labor and are heavy laden, and I will give you rest. (Matthew 11:28)

God, in times of anxiety, I seek Your comforting presence. Reassure me, for Even though I walk through the valley of the shadow of death, I will fear no evil, for you are with me; your rod and your staff, they comfort me. (Psalm 23:4)

Lord J, I pray for Your guidance in managing stress and anxiety effectively. Strengthen me, for Therefore do not worry about tomorrow, for tomorrow will worry about itself. Each day has enough trouble of its own. (Matthew 6:34)

SECTION 3

PRAYERS FOR HEALTHY RELATIONSHIPS

Seeking Discernment In Choosing Friendships And Associations

God, as I choose my friends and associates, I seek Your discernment. Guide me, for Whoever walks with the wise becomes wise, but the companion of fools will suffer harm. (Proverbs 13:20)

Gracious Lord, I pray for Your wisdom in forming associations. Guide my choices, for Do not be deceived: Bad company ruins good morals. (1 Corinthians 15:33)

Almighty God, as I navigate friendships, I ask for Your discernment. Show me the way, for Iron sharpens iron, and one man sharpens another. (Proverbs 27:17)

Lord Jesus, I seek Your wisdom in choosing my associates. Direct my path, for Two are better than one, because they have a good reward for their toil. (Ecclesiastes 4:9)

God of all wisdom, in choosing my friends, I seek Your guidance. Help me to choose wisely, for A friend loves at all times, and a brother is born for adversity. (Proverbs 17:17)

Loving Father, as I form associations, I pray for Your discernment. Guide me, for The righteous choose their friends carefully, but the way of the wicked leads them astray. (Proverbs 12:26)

Merciful God, in selecting my friendships, I seek Your wisdom. Lead me, for A man of many companions may come to ruin, but there is a friend who sticks closer than a brother. (Proverbs 18:24)

Lord Jesus, I pray for Your discernment in forming associations. Guide my decisions, for Do not make friends with a hot-tempered person, do not associate with one easily angered. (Proverbs 22:24)

Seeking Discernment In Choosing Friendships And Associations

God, as I choose my friends, I seek Your wisdom. Direct my choices, for Wounds from a friend can be trusted, but an enemy multiplies kisses. (Proverbs 27:6)

Lord Jesus, I pray for Your discernment in choosing my associates. Enlighten me, for As for the saints in the land, they are the excellent ones, in whom is all my delight. (Psalm 16:3)

Praying For Healthy Relationships With Classmates And Peers

Lord Jesus, I pray for Your blessings on my relationships with my classmates. Strengthen them, for Above all, love each other deeply, because love covers over a multitude of sins. (1 Peter 4:8)

God, I seek Your wisdom in fostering good relations with my peers. Guide me, for By this everyone will know that you are my disciples, if you love one another. (John 13:35)

Lord Jesus, I pray for Your guidance in maintaining healthy relationships with my classmates. Help me, for As iron sharpens iron, so one person sharpens another. (Proverbs 27:17)

Merciful God, as I interact with my peers, I seek Your guidance for healthy relationships. Show me the way, for And as you wish that others would do to you, do so to them. (Luke 6:31)

Praying For Healthy Relationships With Classmates And Peers

God, as I interact with my classmates and peers, I pray for healthy relationships. Guide me, for So whatever you wish that others would do to you, do also to them, for this is the Law and the Prophets. (Matthew 7:12)

Gracious Lord, I seek Your wisdom in building strong relationships with my peers. Help me, for Be completely humble and gentle; be patient, bearing with one another in love. (Ephesians 4:2)

Almighty God, I pray for Your guidance in fostering good relations with my classmates. Show me the way, for A friend loves at all times, and a brother is born for a time of adversity. (Proverbs 17:17)

Lord Jesus, I ask for Your blessings on my relationships with my classmates. Strengthen them, for Bear with each other and forgive one another if any of you has a grievance against someone. Forgive as the Lord forgave you. (Colossians 3:13)

God of all grace, I pray for healthy relationships with my peers. Guide my interactions, for Let no corrupting talk come out of your mouths, but only such as is good for building up, as fits the occasion, that it may give grace to those who hear. (Ephesians 4:29)

Loving Father, I ask for Your wisdom in building strong relationships with my classmates. Guide me, for Therefore encourage one another and build each other up, just as in fact you are doing. (1 Thessalonians 5:11)

Asking For Wisdom In Resolving Conflicts And Misunderstandings

God, as I face conflicts and misunderstandings, I pray for Your wisdom. Guide me, for A soft answer turns away wrath, but a harsh word stirs up anger. (Proverbs 15:1)

Gracious Lord, I seek Your guidance in resolving conflicts. Enlighten me, for Blessed are the peacemakers, for they will be called children of God. (Matthew 5:9)

Almighty God, I ask for Your wisdom in clearing misunderstandings. Lead me, for Strive for peace with everyone, and for the holiness without which no one will see the Lord. (Hebrews 12:14)

Lord Jesus, I pray for Your discernment in dealing with conflicts. Show me the way, for Hatred stirs up strife, but love covers all offenses. (Proverbs 10:12)

God of all understanding, I seek Your guidance in resolving misunderstandings. Help me, for If it is possible, as far as it depends on you, live at peace with everyone. (Romans 12:18)

Loving Father, I pray for Your wisdom in addressing conflicts. Direct me, for Do not repay evil with evil or insult with insult. On the contrary, repay evil with blessing, because to this you were called so that you may inherit a blessing. (1 Peter 3:9)

Merciful God, as I face misunderstandings, I seek Your discernment. Guide me, for Settle matters quickly with your adversary who is taking you to court. Do it while you are still together on the way. (Matthew 5:25)

Asking For Wisdom In Resolving Conflicts And Misunderstandings

God, I ask for Your guidance in clearing misunderstandings. Show me the way, for Therefore, confess your sins to one another and pray for one another, that you may be healed. The prayer of a righteous person has great power as it is working. (James 5:16)

Lord Jesus, I seek Your wisdom in dealing with conflicts. Help me, for Be kind and compassionate to one another, forgiving each other, just as in Christ God forgave you. (Ephesians 4:32)

Lord Jesus, I pray for Your wisdom in resolving conflicts. Enlighten me, for Above all, love each other deeply, because love covers over a multitude of sins. (1 Peter 4:8)

Empathy And Kindness In Interactions With Others

God, I seek Your wisdom to show genuine kindness to others. Enlighten me, for Be completely humble and gentle; be patient, bearing with one another in love. (Ephesians 4:2)

Lord Jesus, I pray for Your grace to be empathetic towards all. Strengthen me, for Whatever you did for one of the least of these brothers and sisters of mine, you did for me. (Matthew 25:40)

Lord Jesus, I ask for Your help to foster empathy in my interactions. Inspire me, for Therefore, as God's chosen people, holy and dearly loved, clothe yourselves with compassion, kindness, humility, gentleness and patience. (Colossians 3:12)

Empathy And Kindness In Interactions With Others

God, as I interact with others, I pray that You instill in me empathy and kindness. Inspire me, for Be kind to one another, tenderhearted, forgiving one another, as God in Christ forgave you. (Ephesians 4:32)

Gracious Lord, I ask for Your guidance in displaying empathy towards others. Mold me, for Rejoice with those who rejoice; mourn with those who mourn. (Romans 12:15)

Almighty God, I seek Your assistance in embodying kindness in my interactions. Guide me, for A gentle answer turns away wrath, but a harsh word stirs up anger. (Proverbs 15:1)

Lord Jesus, I pray for Your help to be empathetic towards others' experiences. Shape me, for Bear one another's burdens, and so fulfill the law of Christ. (Galatians 6:2)

God of all compassion, I seek Your wisdom to show kindness to everyone I meet. Direct me, for But love your enemies, do good to them, and lend to them without expecting to get anything back. Then your reward will be great. (Luke 6:35)

Loving Father, I ask for Your grace to be empathetic in my relationships. Teach me, for Finally, all of you, be like-minded, be sympathetic, love one another, be compassionate and humble. (1 Peter 3:8)

Merciful God, I pray for Your guidance in demonstrating kindness consistently. Guide me, for Do not withhold good from those to whom it is due, when it is in your power to act. (Proverbs 3:27)

Requesting Guidance In Resisting Negative Peer Pressure

God, I pray for Your guidance to resist negative peer pressure. Empower me, for Do not be conformed to this world, but be transformed by the renewal of your mind. (Romans 12:2)

Gracious Lord, I seek Your strength to stand against wrong influences. Support me, for Blessed is the one who does not walk in step with the wicked or stand in the way that sinners take. (Psalm 1:1)

Almighty God, I ask for Your wisdom to discern and resist negative peer pressure. Guide me, for Do not be misled: Bad company corrupts good character. (1 Corinthians 15:33)

Lord Jesus, I pray for Your courage to stand strong against negative influences. Inspire me, for Be strong and courageous. Do not be afraid or terrified because of them, for the Lord your God goes with you; he will never leave you nor forsake you. (Deuteronomy 31:6)

God of all strength, I seek Your guidance in resisting the pressures of wrong company. Protect me, for Keep me from the way of deceit; graciously teach me your law. (Psalm 119:29)

Loving Father, I ask for Your discernment to distinguish and resist negative peer pressure. Enlighten me, for The fear of man lays a snare, but whoever trusts in the Lord is safe. (Proverbs 29:25)

Merciful God, I pray for Your protection from harmful influences. Shield me, for Therefore put on the full armor of God, so that when the day of evil comes, you may be able to stand your ground. (Ephesians 6:13)

Requesting Guidance In Resisting Negative Peer Pressure

God, I seek Your wisdom to resist wrong influences. Guide me, for But test everything; hold fast what is good. Abstain from every form of evil. (1 Thessalonians 5:21-22)

Lord Jesus, I pray for Your strength to resist negative peer pressure. Empower me, for Stand firm then, with the belt of truth buckled around your waist, with the breastplate of righteousness in place. (Ephesians 6:14)

Lord Jesus, I ask for Your guidance to stand firm against negative peer pressure. Strengthen me, for I can do all things through Christ who strengthens me. (Philippians 4:13)

Praying For Courage To Stand Up For One's Values And Beliefs

Lord Jesus, I seek Your strength to remain steadfast in my values and beliefs. Embolden me, for Therefore, since we have such a hope, we are very bold. (2 Corinthians 3:12)

God, I ask for Your courage to stand up for righteousness. Equip me, for So I will always remind you of these things, even though you know them and are firmly established in the truth you now have. (2 Peter 1:12)

Lord Jesus, I pray for Your help in standing firm for my values and beliefs. Strengthen my resolve, for Finally, be strong in the Lord and in his mighty power. (Ephesians 6:10)

Praying For Courage To Stand Up For One's Values And Beliefs

God, I pray for the courage to stand up for my values and beliefs. Strengthen me, for Be strong and courageous. Do not be afraid or terrified because of them, for the LORD your God goes with you; he will never leave you nor forsake you. (Deuteronomy 31:6)

Gracious Lord, I seek Your guidance in standing firm for what I believe. Empower me, for Have I not commanded you? Be strong and courageous. Do not be afraid; do not be discouraged, for the LORD your God will be with you wherever you go. (Joshua 1:9)

Almighty God, I ask for Your courage to uphold my values and beliefs in the face of opposition. Encourage me, for But in your hearts revere Christ as Lord. Always be prepared to give an answer to everyone who asks you to give the reason for the hope that you have. (1 Peter 3:15)

Lord Jesus, I pray for Your strength to stand up for what I believe is right. Inspire me, for Be on your guard; stand firm in the faith; be courageous; be strong. (1 Corinthians 16:13)

God of truth, I seek Your wisdom to boldly defend my values and beliefs. Guide me, for For I am not ashamed of the gospel, because it is the power of God that brings salvation to everyone who believes. (Romans 1:16)

Loving Father, I ask for Your courage to stand up for my convictions. Grant me boldness, for The righteous are as bold as a lion. (Proverbs 28:1)

Merciful God, I pray for Your guidance in standing up for my values and beliefs. Uphold me, for Let your light shine before others, that they may see your good deeds and glorify your Father in heaven. (Matthew 5:16)

Seeking Support In Building A Strong Support Network

God, as I seek to build a strong support network, I pray for Your guidance. Connect me with the right people, for Two are better than one because they have a good reward for their toil. (Ecclesiastes 4:9)

Gracious Lord, I ask for Your wisdom in finding a supportive community. Lead me to those who uplift and encourage, for Iron sharpens iron, and one man sharpens another. (Proverbs 27:17)

Almighty God, I pray for Your guidance in building a strong support network. Surround me with individuals who inspire growth, for Walk with the wise and become wise, for a companion of fools suffers harm. (Proverbs 13:20)

Lord Jesus, I seek Your help in establishing a supportive community. Connect me with like-minded individuals, for Do not be misled: Bad company corrupts good character. (1 Corinthians 15:33)

God of all comfort, I ask for Your guidance in finding a strong support network. Lead me to those who offer solace and encouragement, for Praise be to the God and Father of our Lord Jesus Christ, the Father of compassion and the God of all comfort, who comforts us in all our troubles. (2 Corinthians 1:3-4)

Loving Father, I pray for Your wisdom in building a strong support network. Surround me with individuals who provide guidance and understanding, for Listen to advice and accept discipline, and at the end you will be counted among the wise. (Proverbs 19:20)

Merciful God, as I seek support in my journey, I ask for Your guidance. Connect me with individuals who demonstrate empathy and compassion, for Be kind and compassionate to one another, forgiving each other, just as in Christ God forgave you. (Ephesians 4:32)

Seeking Support In Building A Strong Support Network

Lord Jesus, I pray for Your help in building a strong support network. Lead me to those who offer love and acceptance, for Above all, love each other deeply, because love covers over a multitude of sins. (1 Peter 4:8)

God, I seek Your guidance in establishing a supportive community. Connect me with individuals who share my values and provide encouragement, for Therefore encourage one another and build one another up. (1 Thessalonians 5:11)

Lord Jesus, I pray for Your wisdom in building a strong support network. Surround me with individuals who inspire me to grow and serve You, for Let us consider how we may spur one another on toward love and good deeds. (Hebrews 10:24)

SECTION 4

PRAYERS FOR TIME MANAGEMENT

Asking For Guidance In Making Wise Social Decisions

God, as I navigate social decisions, I seek Your guidance. Direct me, for Trust in the LORD with all your heart, and do not lean on your own understanding. (Proverbs 3:5)

Gracious Lord, I ask for Your wisdom in making wise social choices. Illuminate my path, for The fear of the LORD is the beginning of wisdom, and knowledge of the Holy One is understanding. (Proverbs 9:10)

Almighty God, I pray for Your discernment in making sound social decisions. Guide me, for Walk with the wise and become wise, for a companion of fools suffers harm. (Proverbs 13:20)

Lord Jesus, I seek Your guidance in making wise choices in my social interactions. Show me the way, for Do not be misled: 'Bad company corrupts good character.' (1 Corinthians 15:33)

God of all wisdom, I ask for Your insight in making prudent social decisions. Lead me, for Whoever walks with the wise becomes wise, but the companion of fools will suffer harm. (Proverbs 13:20)

Loving Father, I pray for Your discernment in choosing my social engagements. Inspire me, for Let all that you do be done in love. (1 Corinthians 16:14)

Merciful God, I seek Your guidance in making wise social choices. Help me to discern the right path, for In all your ways acknowledge him, and he will make straight your paths. (Proverbs 3:6)

Asking For Guidance In Making Wise Social Decisions

God, as I navigate social situations, I pray for Your guidance in making wise choices. Lead me, for A man of many companions may come to ruin, but there is a friend who sticks closer than a brother. (Proverbs 18:24)

Lord Jesus, I seek Your wisdom in making wise social decisions. Grant me discernment and understanding, for The way of the righteous is like the first gleam of dawn, which shines ever brighter until the full light of day. (Proverbs 4:18)

Lord Jesus, I ask for Your wisdom in my social decisions. Enlighten me, for By wisdom a house is built, and by understanding it is established. (Proverbs 24:3)

Praying For Discipline And Self-Control In Managing Time

God, I pray for Your guidance in developing discipline and self-control to manage my time wisely. Strengthen my resolve, for So teach us to number our days that we may get a heart of wisdom. (Psalm 90:12)

Gracious Lord, I seek Your help in cultivating discipline and self-control in managing my time. Grant me the ability to prioritize effectively, for But seek first the kingdom of God and his righteousness, and all these things will be added to you. (Matthew 6:33)

Almighty God, I ask for Your grace to develop discipline and self-control in managing my time. Grant me the wisdom to make the most of every opportunity, for Look carefully then how you walk, not as unwise but as wise, making the best use of the time because the days are evil. (Ephesians 5:15-16)

Lord Jesus, I pray for Your guidance in cultivating discipline and self-control to manage my time effectively. Help me to set boundaries and avoid distractions, for Let your speech always be gracious, seasoned with salt, so that you may know how you ought to answer each person. (Colossians 4:6)

God of all wisdom, I seek Your help in developing discipline and self-control to manage my time efficiently. Grant me the ability to manage my tasks and responsibilities with diligence, for Whatever you do, work at it with all your heart, as working for the Lord, not for human masters. (Colossians 3:23)

Praying For Discipline And Self-Control In Managing Time

Loving Father, I ask for Your grace to develop discipline and self-control in managing my time wisely. Help me to prioritize my commitments and make space for what truly matters, for The plans of the diligent lead surely to abundance, but everyone who is hasty comes only to poverty. (Proverbs 21:5)

Merciful God, I pray for Your guidance in cultivating discipline and self-control in managing my time. Help me to overcome procrastination and make productive use of each moment, for Do not love sleep or you will grow poor; stay awake and you will have food to spare. (Proverbs 20:13)

Lord Jesus, I seek Your help in developing discipline and self-control to manage my time effectively. Grant me the ability to establish healthy routines and make wise decisions about my priorities, for But be doers of the word, and not hearers only, deceiving yourselves. (James 1:22)

God, I ask for Your grace to develop discipline and self-control in managing my time. Grant me the strength to resist distractions and focus on the tasks at hand, for Finally, brothers and sisters, whatever is true, whatever is noble, whatever is right, whatever is pure, whatever is lovely, whatever is admirable—if anything is excellent or praiseworthy—think about such things. (Philippians 4:8)

Lord Jesus, I pray for Your guidance in cultivating discipline and self-control in managing my time wisely. Help me to use my time purposefully and to allocate it according to Your will, for Teach us to use wisely all the time we have. (Psalm 90:12, GNT)

Asking For Guidance In Setting Realistic Goals And Expectations

God, I pray for Your guidance in setting realistic goals and expectations. Grant me the wisdom to discern what is attainable, for Commit your work to the LORD, and your plans will be established. (Proverbs 16:3)

Gracious Lord, I seek Your help in setting realistic goals and expectations. Lead me to set objectives that align with Your purpose for my life, for For I know the plans I have for you, declares the LORD, plans for welfare and not for evil, to give you a future and a hope. (Jeremiah 29:11)

Almighty God, I ask for Your wisdom to set realistic goals and expectations. Help me to consider my strengths, limitations, and the resources available to me, for The heart of man plans his way, but the LORD establishes his steps. (Proverbs 16:9)

Lord Jesus, I pray for Your guidance in setting realistic goals and expectations. Help me to be mindful of the journey and embrace the process, for The plans of the diligent lead surely to abundance, but everyone who is hasty comes only to poverty. (Proverbs 21:5)

God of all wisdom, I seek Your help in setting realistic goals and expectations. Grant me the ability to prioritize and allocate my time and energy wisely, for But seek first the kingdom of God and his righteousness, and all these things will be added to you. (Matthew 6:33)

Loving Father, I ask for Your grace to set realistic goals and expectations. Help me to embrace growth and progress rather than perfection, for I press on toward the goal for the prize of the upward call of God in Christ Jesus. (Philippians 3:14)

Asking For Guidance In Setting Realistic Goals And Expectations

Merciful God, I pray for Your guidance in setting realistic goals and expectations. Help me to find balance and avoid setting unattainable standards, for Let all that you do be done in love. (1 Corinthians 16:14)

Lord Jesus, I seek Your wisdom in setting realistic goals and expectations. Grant me the ability to break them down into smaller, achievable steps, for The plans of the diligent lead surely to abundance, but everyone who is hasty comes only to poverty. (Proverbs 21:5)

God, I ask for Your guidance in setting realistic goals and expectations. Help me to be patient and flexible, surrendering to Your timing and purpose, for But they who wait for the LORD shall renew their strength; they shall mount up with wings like eagles. (Isaiah 40:31)

Lord Jesus, I pray for Your wisdom and guidance in setting realistic goals and expectations. Help me to align them with Your will and trust in Your perfect timing, for Commit your way to the LORD; trust in him, and he will act. (Psalm 37:5)

Praying For Effective Strategies To Manage Procrastination

God, I pray for Your guidance in overcoming procrastination. Grant me the discipline and motivation to take action, for Do not be slothful in zeal, be fervent in spirit, serve the Lord. (Romans 12:11)

Gracious Lord, I seek Your help in managing procrastination. Give me the strength to resist distractions and the wisdom to prioritize my tasks, for Whatever you do, work heartily, as for the Lord and not for men. (Colossians 3:23)

Almighty God, I ask for Your grace to overcome procrastination. Help me to break tasks into manageable steps and set realistic deadlines, for The plans of the diligent lead surely to abundance, but everyone who is hasty comes only to poverty. (Proverbs 21:5)

Lord Jesus, I pray for Your guidance in managing procrastination. Grant me the ability to overcome perfectionism and fear of failure, for Trust in the LORD with all your heart, and do not lean on your own understanding. (Proverbs 3:5)

God of all wisdom, I seek Your help in developing effective strategies to manage procrastination. Grant me the discipline to set aside dedicated time for focused work, for He who gathers in summer is a prudent son, but he who sleeps in harvest is a son who brings shame. (Proverbs 10:5)

Loving Father, I ask for Your grace to conquer procrastination. Help me to cultivate a mindset of productivity and to establish healthy routines, for Be very careful, then, how you live—not as unwise but as wise. (Ephesians 5:15)

Praying For Effective Strategies To Manage Procrastination

Merciful God, I pray for Your guidance in managing procrastination. Help me to identify and address the underlying reasons for my delay, for Create in me a clean heart, O God, and renew a right spirit within me. (Psalm 51:10)

Lord Jesus, I seek Your help in overcoming procrastination. Grant me the ability to focus on the task at hand and to resist the allure of immediate gratification, for But seek first the kingdom of God and his righteousness, and all these things will be added to you. (Matthew 6:33)

God, I ask for Your wisdom to develop effective strategies to manage procrastination. Guide me to use tools and techniques that promote productivity and time management, for For everything there is a season, and a time for every matter under heaven. (Ecclesiastes 3:1)

Lord Jesus, I pray for Your intervention in managing procrastination. Help me to find accountability and support in my journey toward overcoming this challenge, for Iron sharpens iron, and one man sharpens another. (Proverbs 27:17)

Seeking Wisdom In Planning Study Schedules And Routine

God, I pray for Your guidance in planning my study schedules and routines. Grant me the wisdom to allocate my time wisely, for Teach us to number our days, that we may gain a heart of wisdom. (Psalm 90:12)

Gracious Lord, I seek Your help in creating effective study schedules and routines. Give me the insight to prioritize my tasks and establish a balance between work and rest, for For everything there is a season, and a time for every matter under heaven. (Ecclesiastes 3:1)

Almighty God, I ask for Your wisdom in planning my study schedules and routines. Help me to set realistic goals and break them down into manageable tasks, for Commit to the LORD whatever you do, and he will establish your plans. (Proverbs 16:3)

Lord Jesus, I pray for Your guidance in designing effective study schedules and routines. Grant me the discipline to stick to my plan and the ability to adapt when necessary, for Trust in the LORD with all your heart, and do not lean on your own understanding. (Proverbs 3:5)

God of all wisdom, I seek Your help in creating study schedules and routines that align with Your purpose for my life. Lead me to prioritize my studies in a way that honors You, for But seek first the kingdom of God and his righteousness, and all these things will be added to you. (Matthew 6:33)

Loving Father, I ask for Your grace to plan my study schedules and routines wisely. Help me to establish a structure that fosters focus, productivity, and balance, for Let all things be done decently and in order. (1 Corinthians 14:40)

Seeking Wisdom In Planning Study Schedules And Routine

Merciful God, I pray for Your guidance in mapping out effective study schedules and routines. Grant me the ability to create a conducive environment and eliminate distractions, for And whatever you do, in word or deed, do everything in the name of the Lord Jesus, giving thanks to God the Father through him. (Colossians 3:17)

Lord Jesus, I seek Your help in planning my study schedules and routines. Grant me the wisdom to identify my most productive times and allocate them to focused study, for Whatever you do, work heartily, as for the Lord and not for men. (Colossians 3:23)

God, I ask for Your wisdom in designing study schedules and routines that support my learning and growth. Help me to embrace consistency and perseverance in my studies, for Let us not become weary in doing good, for at the proper time we will reap a harvest if we do not give up. (Galatians 6:9)

Lord Jesus, I pray for Your guidance in planning my study schedules and routines. Grant me the discernment to recognize when to rest and rejuvenate, for He gives power to the faint, and to him who has no might he increases strength. (Isaiah 40:29)

SECTION 5

PRAYERS FOR FRIENDSHIPS

Seeking Genuine And Supportive Friendships

God, I pray for Your guidance in seeking genuine and supportive friendships. Lead me to connect with individuals who will uplift and encourage me, for A friend loves at all times, and a brother is born for a time of adversity. (Proverbs 17:17)

Gracious Lord, I seek Your help in cultivating genuine and supportive friendships. Bring people into my life who will walk alongside me in faith and love, for Two are better than one because they have a good reward for their toil. (Ecclesiastes 4:9)

Almighty God, I ask for Your grace to find genuine and supportive friendships. Surround me with friends who share my values and inspire growth, for Do not be misled: Bad company corrupts good character. (1 Corinthians 15:33)

Lord Jesus, I pray for Your guidance in developing genuine and supportive friendships. Help me to be a true friend to others and attract those who will reciprocate, for A man of many companions may come to ruin, but there is a friend who sticks closer than a brother. (Proverbs 18:24)

God of all compassion, I seek Your intervention in finding genuine and supportive friendships. Lead me to those who will offer understanding, acceptance, and encouragement, for A friend loves at all times, and a brother is born for adversity. (Proverbs 17:17)

Loving Father, I ask for Your help in building genuine and supportive friendships. Grant me the ability to foster meaningful connections based on mutual respect and care, for Love one another with brotherly affection. Outdo one another in showing honor. (Romans 12:10)

Seeking Genuine And Supportive Friendships

Merciful God, I pray for Your guidance in seeking genuine and supportive friendships. Help me to discern true companionship from superficial relationships, for Whoever walks with the wise becomes wise, but the companion of fools will suffer harm. (Proverbs 13:20)

Lord Jesus, I seek Your assistance in finding genuine and supportive friendships. Lead me to individuals who will uplift my spirit and spur me on in my journey of faith, for As iron sharpens iron, so one person sharpens another. (Proverbs 27:17)

God, I ask for Your wisdom in cultivating genuine and supportive friendships. Help me to be vulnerable and open to meaningful connections, for Therefore encourage one another and build one another up. (1 Thessalonians 5:11)

Lord Jesus, I pray for Your intervention in finding genuine and supportive friendships. Guide me to friends who will share my joys and sorrows, and together we can grow in love and righteousness, for A sweet friendship refreshes the soul. (Proverbs 27:9, MSG)

Praying For Understanding And Acceptance From Friends

God, I pray for understanding and acceptance from my friends. Help them to see my heart and accept me for who I am, for Accept one another, then, just as Christ accepted you, in order to bring praise to God. (Romans 15:7)

Gracious Lord, I seek Your guidance in fostering understanding and acceptance among my friends. Soften their hearts to empathize with my struggles and celebrate my joys, for Bear one another's burdens, and so fulfill the law of Christ. (Galatians 6:2)

Almighty God, I ask for Your grace in promoting understanding and acceptance within my friendships. Help my friends to embrace our differences and appreciate the unique qualities we each bring, for Love is patient and kind; love does not envy or boast; it is not arrogant. (1 Corinthians 13:4)

Lord Jesus, I pray for Your divine intervention in bringing understanding and acceptance among my friends. Open their minds to see beyond surface-level differences and recognize the value we each bring to the relationship, for For we are all one in Christ Jesus. (Galatians 3:28)

God of all comfort, I seek Your intervention in fostering understanding and acceptance among my friends. Help them to extend grace and forgiveness, as we all fall short at times, for Above all, keep loving one another earnestly, since love covers a multitude of sins. (1 Peter 4:8)

Praying For Understanding And Acceptance From Friends

Merciful God, I pray for Your guidance in cultivating understanding and acceptance among my friends. Help them to see the beauty of our shared experiences and the strength that comes from embracing diversity, for Have unity of mind, sympathy, brotherly love, a tender heart, and a humble mind. (1 Peter 3:8)

Lord Jesus, I seek Your help in promoting understanding and acceptance among my friends. Inspire them to love unconditionally, just as You have loved us, for By this all people will know that you are my disciples if you have love for one another. (John 13:35)

God, I ask for Your wisdom in fostering understanding and acceptance among my friendships. Help my friends to see the goodness in my intentions and grant me the grace to extend the same to them, for Let all that you do be done in love. (1 Corinthians 16:14)

Lord Jesus, I pray for Your divine intervention in fostering understanding and acceptance among my friends. Help us to build a foundation of trust, empathy, and unconditional love, for Above all, keep loving one another earnestly, since love covers a multitude of sins. (1 Peter 4:8)

Loving Father, I ask for Your grace to promote understanding and acceptance within my friendships. Guide my friends to listen with compassion and seek to understand before passing judgment, for Let every person be quick to hear, slow to speak, slow to anger. (James 1:19)

Asking For Guidance In Resolving Conflicts Within Friendships

God, I pray for Your guidance in resolving conflicts within my friendships. Grant us the humility to listen, the wisdom to understand, and the grace to forgive, for If possible, so far as it depends on you, live peaceably with all. (Romans 12:18)

Gracious Lord, I seek Your help in navigating conflicts within my friendships. Give us the courage to address the issues with love and respect, seeking reconciliation and restoration, for Blessed are the peacemakers, for they shall be called sons of God. (Matthew 5:9)

Almighty God, I ask for Your grace in resolving conflicts within my friendships. Help us to communicate honestly and openly, seeking understanding and finding common ground, for Let each of you look not only to his own interests but also to the interests of others. (Philippians 2:4)

Lord Jesus, I pray for Your intervention in healing the conflicts within my friendships. Guide us to approach each other with kindness, empathy, and a desire for reconciliation, for Put on then, as God's chosen ones, holy and beloved, compassionate hearts, kindness, humility, meekness, and patience. (Colossians 3:12)

God of all peace, I seek Your wisdom in resolving conflicts within my friendships. Help us to seek solutions that promote understanding, forgiveness, and growth in our relationships, for If your brother sins against you, go and tell him his fault, between you and him alone. (Matthew 18:15)

Asking For Guidance In Resolving Conflicts Within Friendships

Merciful God, I pray for Your guidance in resolving conflicts within my friendships. Help us to embrace forgiveness, letting go of resentment and fostering reconciliation, for Bearing with one another and, if one has a complaint against another, forgiving each other; as the Lord has forgiven you, so you also must forgive. (Colossians 3:13)

Lord Jesus, I seek Your help in resolving conflicts within my friendships. Grant us the patience to listen, the wisdom to find common ground, and the love to restore and strengthen our bonds, for By this all people will know that you are my disciples, if you have love for one another. (John 13:35)

God, I ask for Your wisdom in navigating conflicts within my friendships. Help us to approach resolution with humility, seeking understanding and reconciliation, for Good sense makes one slow to anger, and it is his glory to overlook an offense. (Proverbs 19:11)

Lord Jesus, I pray for Your divine intervention in resolving conflicts within my friendships. Grant us the guidance to communicate effectively, the patience to listen attentively, and the grace to extend forgiveness, for And above all these put on love, which binds everything together in perfect harmony. (Colossians 3:14)

Loving Father, I ask for Your grace to navigate the conflicts within my friendships. Grant us the ability to empathize with one another's perspectives and to approach the resolution process with a spirit of humility and grace, for Be kind to one another, tenderhearted, forgiving one another, as God in Christ forgave you. (Ephesians 4:32)

Forgiveness And Reconciliation In Strained Relationships

God, I pray for the power of forgiveness and reconciliation in strained relationships. Soften our hearts and help us to let go of resentment, for Be kind to one another, tenderhearted, forgiving one another, as God in Christ forgave you. (Ephesians 4:32)

Gracious Lord, I seek Your help in healing strained relationships through forgiveness and reconciliation. Guide us to humbly seek restoration, for If possible, so far as it depends on you, live peaceably with all. (Romans 12:18)

Almighty God, I ask for Your grace to invoke forgiveness and reconciliation in strained relationships. Grant us the courage to extend forgiveness and the desire for peaceful resolution, for And whenever you stand praying, forgive, if you have anything against anyone, so that your Father also who is in heaven may forgive you your trespasses. (Mark 11:25)

Lord Jesus, I pray for Your intervention in strained relationships, bringing about forgiveness and reconciliation. Help us to release the burden of grudges and restore harmony, for Bear with each other and forgive one another if any of you has a grievance against someone. Forgive as the Lord forgave you. (Colossians 3:13)

God of all mercy, I seek Your guidance in forgiveness and reconciliation in strained relationships. Enable us to extend grace and seek understanding, for Put on then, as God's chosen ones, holy and beloved, compassionate hearts, kindness, humility, meekness, and patience. (Colossians 3:12)

Forgiveness And Reconciliation In Strained Relationships

Loving Father, I ask for Your help in forgiveness and reconciliation in strained relationships. Grant us the wisdom to communicate with love and seek reconciliation, for So if you are offering your gift at the altar and there remember that your brother has something against you, leave your gift there before the altar and go. First, be reconciled to your brother, and then come and offer your gift. (Matthew 5:23-24)

Merciful God, I pray for Your intervention in strained relationships, forgiveness and reconciliation. Help us to let go of past hurts and extend grace to one another, for For if you forgive others their trespasses, your God will also forgive you. (Matthew 6:14)

Lord Jesus, I seek Your divine intervention in strained relationships, forgiveness and reconciliation. Grant us the humility to seek forgiveness and the willingness to forgive, for But I say to you, Love your enemies and pray for those who persecute you. (Matthew 5:44)

God, I ask for Your grace in forgiveness and reconciliation in strained relationships. Lead us to have open hearts, ready to reconcile and restore broken bonds, for And above all these put on love, which binds everything together in perfect harmony. (Colossians 3:14)

Lord Jesus, I pray for Your divine intervention in strained relationships, forgiveness and reconciliation. Help us to follow Your example of forgiveness and love, for And be kind to one another, tenderhearted, forgiving one another, even as God in Christ forgave you. (Ephesians 4:32)

Requesting Wisdom In Nurturing Healthy Friendships

God, I pray for Your wisdom in nurturing healthy friendships. Guide me in choosing friends who will inspire, encourage, and uplift me, for Whoever walks with the wise becomes wise, but the companion of fools will suffer harm. (Proverbs 13:20)

Gracious Lord, I seek Your help in cultivating healthy friendships. Grant me discernment to invest in relationships that are rooted in love, respect, and shared values, for A friend loves at all times and a brother is born for a time of adversity. (Proverbs 17:17)

Almighty God, I ask for Your grace to nurture healthy friendships. Help me to be a faithful and supportive friend, and to surround myself with those who will challenge me to grow in righteousness, for Iron sharpens iron, and one man sharpens another. (Proverbs 27:17)

Lord Jesus, I pray for Your guidance in nurturing healthy friendships. Grant me the wisdom to set healthy boundaries, to communicate effectively, and to cultivate trust and vulnerability, for A man of many companions may come to ruin, but there is a friend who sticks closer than a brother. (Proverbs 18:24)

God of all compassion, I seek Your help in nurturing healthy friendships. Teach me to love my friends unconditionally, to listen attentively, and to offer support and understanding, for Above all, keep loving one another earnestly, since love covers a multitude of sins. (1 Peter 4:8)

Loving Father, I ask for Your grace to nurture healthy friendships. Help me to prioritize quality over quantity, investing my time and energy in building deep and meaningful connections, for Do to others as you would have them do to you. (Luke 6:31)

Requesting Wisdom In Nurturing Healthy Friendships

Merciful God, I pray for Your guidance in nurturing healthy friendships. Grant me the wisdom to choose friends who will bring out the best in me and help me to grow in faith and character, for As iron sharpens iron, so one person sharpens another. (Proverbs 27:17)

Lord Jesus, I seek Your help in nurturing healthy friendships. Teach me to be patient, understanding, and forgiving, and to foster an environment of mutual respect and support, for Be kind to one another, tenderhearted, forgiving one another, as God in Christ forgave you. (Ephesians 4:32)

God, I ask for Your wisdom to nurture healthy friendships. Grant me the ability to celebrate the successes of my friends, to offer a shoulder to lean on in times of trouble, and to be a source of encouragement and inspiration, for A sweet friendship refreshes the soul. (Proverbs 27:9, MSG)

Lord Jesus, I pray for Your divine intervention in nurturing healthy friendships. Help me to be a true friend, embodying love, loyalty, and authenticity, for This is my commandment, that you love one another as I have loved you. (John 15:12)

Praying For Loyalty And Trust In Friendships

God, I pray for loyalty and trust in my friendships. Grant me the ability to be a trustworthy friend and to attract loyal companions, for Let love and faithfulness never leave you; bind them around your neck, write them on the tablet of your heart. (Proverbs 3:3)

Gracious Lord, I seek Your help in cultivating loyalty and trust in my friendships. Guide me to choose friends who are reliable, honest, and committed, for The heartfelt counsel of a friend is as sweet as perfume and incense. (Proverbs 27:9, NLT)

Almighty God, I ask for Your grace to foster loyalty and trust in my friendships. Help me to be a friend who keeps confidence, offers support without judgment, and remains steadfast through the ups and downs, for A friend loves at all times, and a brother is born for a time of adversity. (Proverbs 17:17)

Lord Jesus, I pray for Your intervention in nurturing loyalty and trust in my friendships. Grant me the discernment to surround myself with friends who are faithful and trustworthy, for Better is open rebuke than hidden love. Faithful are the wounds of a friend; profuse are the kisses of an enemy. (Proverbs 27:5-6)

God of all faithfulness, I seek Your help in cultivating loyalty and trust in my friendships. Teach me to be a friend who stands by others in both joy and sorrow, for A friend is always loyal, and a brother is born to help in time of need. (Proverbs 17:17, NLT)

Loving Father, I ask for Your grace to foster loyalty and trust in my friendships. Help me to be a friend who is reliable, dependable, and true to my word, for Let what you say be simply 'Yes' or 'No'; anything more than this comes from evil. (Matthew 5:37)

Praying For Loyalty And Trust In Friendships

Merciful God, I pray for Your guidance in nurturing loyalty and trust in my friendships. Grant me the wisdom to build a foundation of open communication, honesty, and mutual respect, for Do not withhold good from those to whom it is due when it is in your power to do it. (Proverbs 3:27)

Lord Jesus, I seek Your help in fostering loyalty and trust in my friendships. Teach me to forgive and extend grace when trust is broken, and to offer second chances, for Above all, keep loving one another earnestly, since love covers a multitude of sins. (1 Peter 4:8)

God, I ask for Your wisdom in cultivating loyalty and trust in my friendships. Help me to be a friend who encourages and believes in others, fostering an environment of safety and reliability, for Therefore encourage one another and build one another up, just as you are doing. (1 Thessalonians 5:11)

Lord Jesus, I pray for Your divine intervention in fostering loyalty and trust in my friendships. Grant me the ability to be loyal and trustworthy, and to attract friends who demonstrate the same qualities, for Whoever pursues righteousness and kindness will find life, righteousness, and honor. (Proverbs 21:21)

SEEKING COMPANIONSHIP AND ENCOURAGEMENT FROM FRIENDS

God, I pray for companionship and encouragement from my friends. Surround me with friends who will walk beside me, offering support, love, and companionship, for Two are better than one because they have a good return for their labor. (Ecclesiastes 4:9)

Gracious Lord, I seek Your help in finding companionship and encouragement from my friends. Bring people into my life who will uplift me, speak truth into my life, and provide a listening ear, for Oil and perfume make the heart glad, and the sweetness of a friend comes from his earnest counsel. (Proverbs 27:9)

Almighty God, I ask for Your grace to find companionship and encouragement from my friends. Help us to be sources of strength and inspiration for one another, offering support and comfort in times of need, for Therefore encourage one another and build one another up, just as you are doing. (1 Thessalonians 5:11)

Lord Jesus, I pray for Your intervention in seeking companionship and encouragement from my friends. Grant me the wisdom to cultivate deep and meaningful connections, where we can lean on each other and find solace in difficult times, for Carry each other's burdens, and in this way, you will fulfill the law of Christ. (Galatians 6:2)

God of all comfort, I seek Your help in finding companionship and encouragement from my friends. Lead me to those who will offer love, understanding, and a sense of belonging, for A friend loves at all times and a brother is born for a time of adversity. (Proverbs 17:17)

Seeking Companionship And Encouragement From Friends

Loving Father, I ask for Your grace to seek companionship and encouragement from my friends. Help me to foster an environment of vulnerability and authenticity, where we can share our joys and sorrows, for Rejoice with those who rejoice, weep with those who weep. (Romans 12:15)

Merciful God, I pray for Your guidance in seeking companionship and encouragement from my friends. Grant me the ability to be a friend who offers unwavering support, empathy, and encouragement, for A sweet friendship refreshes the soul. (Proverbs 27:9, MSG)

Lord Jesus, I seek Your help in finding companionship and encouragement from my friends. Teach us to be a community that spurs one another on toward love and good deeds, for And let us consider how to stir up one another to love and good works. (Hebrews 10:24)

God, I ask for Your wisdom to seek companionship and encouragement from my friends. Lead us to create an atmosphere of love, acceptance, and positivity, where we can inspire and uplift one another, for Therefore encourage one another and build one another up, just as you are doing. (1 Thessalonians 5:11)

Lord Jesus, I pray for Your divine intervention in seeking companionship and encouragement from my friends. Help us to walk together in unity, supporting and motivating one another to live out our God-given purpose, for Iron sharpens iron, and one person sharpens another. (Proverbs 27:17)

SECTION 6

PRAYERS DURING CHALLENGING TIMES

Asking For Divine Intervention In Finding Like-Minded Peers

God, I pray for divine intervention in finding like-minded peers. Lead me to those who share my values, passions, and aspirations, for Do not be unequally yoked with unbelievers. For what partnership has righteousness with lawlessness? Or what fellowship has light with darkness? (2 Corinthians 6:14)

Gracious Lord, I seek Your help in connecting with like-minded peers. Guide me to individuals who will understand and support my journey, for Make me to know your ways, O LORD; teach me your paths. (Psalm 25:4)

Almighty God, I ask for Your grace to bring like-minded peers into my life. Help me to find companions who will encourage and inspire me to grow in faith and purpose, for Whoever walks with the wise becomes wise, but the companion of fools will suffer harm. (Proverbs 13:20)

Lord Jesus, I pray for Your intervention in finding like-minded peers. Surround me with friends who will walk alongside me in righteousness, pursuing Your truth and glorifying Your name, for The righteous choose their friends carefully, but the way of the wicked leads them astray. (Proverbs 12:26)

God of all wisdom, I seek Your help in connecting with like-minded peers. Lead me to those who share my passion for Your Word and desire to live according to Your will, for Iron sharpens iron, and one man sharpens another. (Proverbs 27:17)

Loving Father, I ask for Your guidance in finding like-minded peers. Help me to seek companions who will support and challenge me to grow in my relationship with You, for And let us consider how to stir up one another to love and good works. (Hebrews 10:24)

Asking For Divine Intervention In Finding Like-Minded Peers

Merciful God, I pray for Your intervention in bringing like-minded peers into my life. Grant me the discernment to recognize those who align with Your truth and purpose, for For as in one body we have many members, and the members do not all have the same function. (Romans 12:4)

Lord Jesus, I seek Your help in connecting with like-minded peers. Lead me to a community where we can learn, worship, and serve You together, for For where two or three are gathered in my name, there am I among them. (Matthew 18:20)

God, I ask for Your wisdom in finding like-minded peers. Guide me to those who will walk alongside me in faith, providing encouragement and accountability, for And let us not neglect our meeting together, as some people do, but encourage one another, especially now that the day of his return is drawing near. (Hebrews 10:25, NLT)

Lord Jesus, I pray for Your divine intervention in finding like-minded peers. Surround me with individuals who will inspire and challenge me to pursue Your truth and purpose, for As iron sharpens iron, so one person sharpens another. (Proverbs 27:17)

PRAYING FOR RESILIENCE AND DETERMINATION DURING DIFFICULT TIMES

God, I pray for resilience and determination during difficult times. Grant me the strength to endure challenges and the determination to press forward, knowing that You are with me, for I can do all things through him who strengthens me. (Philippians 4:13)

Gracious Lord, I seek Your help in cultivating resilience and determination in the face of adversity. Fill me with unwavering hope and the courage to overcome obstacles, for But they who wait for the LORD shall renew their strength; they shall mount up with wings like eagles; they shall run and not be weary; they shall walk and not faint. (Isaiah 40:31)

Almighty God, I ask for Your grace to invoke resilience and determination during difficult times. Help me to find solace in Your promises, knowing that You are working all things together for my good, for And we know that for those who love God all things work together for good, for those who are called according to his purpose. (Romans 8:28)

Lord Jesus, I pray for Your intervention in fostering resilience and determination in challenging moments. Grant me the perseverance to keep moving forward, even when the path seems uncertain, for Blessed is the man who remains steadfast under trial, for when he has stood the test he will receive the crown of life, which God has promised to those who love him. (James 1:12)

God of all comfort, I seek Your help in finding resilience and determination during difficult times. Remind me of Your faithfulness and the strength that comes from trusting in You, for The LORD is my strength and my shield; in him my heart trusts, and I am helped; my heart exults, and with my song, I give thanks to him. (Psalm 28:7)

Praying For Resilience And Determination During Difficult Times

Loving Father, I ask for Your grace to cultivate resilience and determination in the face of challenges. Fill me with Your peace that surpasses all understanding, strengthening my resolve to persevere, for Peace I leave with you; my peace I give to you. Not as the world gives do I give to you. Let not your hearts be troubled, neither let them be afraid. (John 14:27)

Merciful God, I pray for Your guidance inresilience and determination during difficult times. Help me to find strength in Your Word and to anchor my hope in Your unfailing love, for The LORD is my rock and my fortress and my deliverer, my God, my rock, in whom I take refuge, my shield, and the horn of my salvation, my stronghold. (Psalm 18:2)

Lord Jesus, I seek Your help in fostering resilience and determination in the midst of trials. Teach me to fix my eyes on You, trusting that You are working in and through every circumstance, for Let us run with endurance the race that is set before us, looking to Jesus, the founder and perfecter of our faith. (Hebrews 12:1-2)

God, I ask for Your wisdom in cultivating resilience and determination during difficult times. Grant me the faith to persevere, knowing that Your power is made perfect in weakness, for But he said to me, 'My grace is sufficient for you, for my power is made perfect in weakness.' Therefore, I will boast all the more gladly of my weaknesses, so that the power of Christ may rest upon me. (2 Corinthians 12:9)

Lord Jesus, I pray for Your divine intervention in resilience and determination during difficult times. Help me to lean on Your strength, to rise above challenges, and to trust in Your plan for my life, for I have said these things to you, that in me you may have peace. In the world, you will have tribulation. But take heart; I have overcome the world. (John 16:33)

Asking For Wisdom In Overcoming Academic Setbacks

God, I pray for wisdom in overcoming academic setbacks. Guide me to learn from my mistakes, to grow in resilience, and to find new strategies to succeed, for The fear of the LORD is the beginning of wisdom, and knowledge of the Holy One is understanding. (Proverbs 9:10)

Gracious Lord, I seek Your help in navigating academic setbacks. Grant me the wisdom to persevere, the humility to seek assistance, and the clarity to identify areas for improvement, for For the LORD gives wisdom; from his mouth come knowledge and understanding. (Proverbs 2:6)

Almighty God, I ask for Your grace to overcome academic setbacks. Help me to trust in Your guidance and to find wisdom in the midst of challenges, for If any of you lacks wisdom, let him ask God, who gives generously to all without reproach, and it will be given him. (James 1:5)

Lord Jesus, I pray for Your intervention in overcoming academic setbacks. Grant me the strength to persevere and the discernment to learn from my experiences, for Trust in the LORD with all your heart, and do not lean on your own understanding. (Proverbs 3:5)

God of all knowledge, I seek Your help in overcoming academic setbacks. Open my mind to new insights, creative solutions, and effective study strategies, for For the LORD gives wisdom; from his mouth come knowledge and understanding. (Proverbs 2:6)

Asking For Wisdom In Overcoming Academic Setbacks

Merciful God, I pray for Your guidance in overcoming academic setbacks. Grant me the discernment to seek help when needed, the determination to learn from setbacks, and the wisdom to make necessary adjustments, for Listen to advice and accept instruction, that you may gain wisdom in the future. (Proverbs 19:20)

Lord Jesus, I seek Your help in overcoming academic setbacks. Teach me to embrace failures as opportunities for growth and to rely on Your wisdom and strength to overcome obstacles, for But he said to me, 'My grace is sufficient for you, for my power is made perfect in weakness.' (2 Corinthians 12:9)

God, I ask for Your wisdom to overcome academic setbacks. Help me to approach challenges with resilience, seeking Your guidance and trusting in Your plan for my educational journey, for For I know the plans I have for you, declares the LORD, plans for welfare and not for evil, to give you a future and a hope. (Jeremiah 29:11)

Lord Jesus, I pray for Your divine intervention in overcoming academic setbacks. Grant me the wisdom to persevere, the humility to seek guidance, and the resilience to bounce back stronger, for But the wisdom that comes from heaven is first of all pure; then peace-loving, considerate, submissive, full of mercy and good fruit, impartial and sincere. (James 3:17)

Loving Father, I ask for Your grace to navigate academic setbacks with wisdom. Help me to approach challenges with a growth mindset, knowing that through perseverance and Your guidance, I can overcome obstacles, for I can do all things through him who strengthens me. (Philippians 4:13)

Guidance In Navigating Financial Challenges

God, I pray for guidance in navigating financial challenges. Grant me wisdom to make wise decisions, to steward my resources well, and to seek Your provision and guidance, for Trust in the LORD with all your heart, and do not lean on your own understanding. (Proverbs 3:5)

Gracious Lord, I seek Your help in navigating financial challenges. Guide me to find solutions, to be diligent in managing my finances, and to trust in Your abundance and provision, for And my God will supply every need of yours according to his riches in glory in Christ Jesus. (Philippians 4:19)

Almighty God, I ask for Your grace to overcome financial challenges. Help me to seek Your wisdom and discernment in budgeting, saving, and making financial decisions, for For the LORD gives wisdom; from his mouth come knowledge and understanding. (Proverbs 2:6)

Lord Jesus, I pray for Your intervention in navigating financial challenges. Grant me the courage to seek help when needed, the discipline to manage my resources wisely, and the trust to rely on Your provision, for The LORD is my shepherd; I shall not want. (Psalm 23:1)

God of all provision, I seek Your help in navigating financial challenges. Open doors of opportunity, provide for my needs, and guide me in making wise financial choices, for And without faith, it is impossible to please him, for whoever would draw near to God must believe that he exists and that he rewards those who seek him. (Hebrews 11:6)

Guidance In Navigating Financial Challenges

Merciful God, I pray for Your guidance in overcoming financial challenges. Grant me the wisdom to discern between needs and wants, to be disciplined in budgeting, and to seek opportunities for growth and provision, for But seek first the kingdom of God and his righteousness, and all these things will be added to you. (Matthew 6:33)

Lord Jesus, I seek Your help in navigating financial challenges. Teach me to be content in all circumstances, to be generous with what I have, and to trust in Your guidance and provision, for Each one must give as he has decided in his heart, not reluctantly or under compulsion, for God loves a cheerful giver. (2 Corinthians 9:7)

God, I ask for Your wisdom in navigating financial challenges. Grant me the discernment to make sound financial decisions, to be responsible in managing debts, and to seek Your provision and guidance in all financial matters, for The rich rules over the poor, and the borrower is the slave of the lender. (Proverbs 22:7)

Lord Jesus, I pray for Your divine intervention in navigating financial challenges. Grant me the wisdom to seek counsel, the perseverance to overcome obstacles, and the trust to rely on Your faithfulness, for But seek first the kingdom of God and his righteousness, and all these things will be added to you. (Matthew 6:33)

Loving Father, I ask for Your grace to navigate financial challenges with wisdom. Teach me to be a good steward of the resources You have entrusted to me, to prioritize wisely, and to seek contentment in all circumstances, for Keep your life free from love of money, and be content with what you have, for he has said, 'I will never leave you nor forsake you.' (Hebrews 13:5)

Requesting Divine Intervention In Overcoming Health Issues

God, I pray for divine intervention in overcoming health issues. Grant me physical strength, healing, and restoration, for I will restore health to you, and your wounds I will heal, declares the LORD. (Jeremiah 30:17)

Gracious Lord, I seek Your help in navigating health challenges. Guide the hands of doctors and healthcare professionals, and grant me the wisdom to make wise decisions regarding my health, for For I am the LORD, your God, who takes hold of your right hand and says to you, Do not fear; I will help you. (Isaiah 41:13)

Almighty God, I ask for Your grace to overcome health issues. Fill me with hope, strength, and resilience as I face physical challenges, for But he said to me, 'My grace is sufficient for you, for my power is made perfect in weakness.' (2 Corinthians 12:9)

Lord Jesus, I pray for Your intervention in overcoming health issues. Grant me the peace that surpasses all understanding, knowing that You are with me in my journey toward healing and wholeness, for Peace I leave with you; my peace I give to you. Not as the world gives do I give to you. Let not your hearts be troubled, neither let them be afraid. (John 14:27)

God of all healing, I seek Your help in overcoming health issues. Pour out Your healing touch upon my body, mind, and spirit, and grant me the strength to persevere through the challenges, for But he was pierced for our transgressions; he was crushed for our iniquities; upon him was the chastisement that brought us peace, and with his wounds, we are healed. (Isaiah 53:5)

Requesting Divine Intervention In Overcoming Health Issues

Loving Father, I ask for Your grace to navigate health issues with faith and courage. Help me to trust in Your sovereignty and to find comfort in Your presence, for Even though I walk through the valley of the shadow of death, I will fear no evil, for you are with me; your rod and your staff, they comfort me. (Psalm 23:4)

Merciful God, I pray for Your guidance in overcoming health issues. Grant me the wisdom to make healthy choices, the strength to persevere through treatments, and the trust to surrender my health into Your loving hands, for Beloved, I pray that all may go well with you and that you may be in good health, as it goes well with your soul. (3 John 1:2)

Lord Jesus, I seek Your help in overcoming health issues. Teach me to find peace and healing in Your presence, to trust in Your power to restore, and to embrace the journey toward wholeness, for Heal me, O LORD, and I shall be healed; save me, and I shall be saved, for you are my praise. (Jeremiah 17:14)

God, I ask for Your wisdom in navigating health issues. Grant me the discernment to seek proper care, the patience to endure the healing process, and the faith to believe in Your restoring power, for And the prayer of faith will save the one who is sick, and the Lord will raise him up. (James 5:15)

Lord Jesus, I pray for Your divine intervention in overcoming health issues. Grant me strength, resilience, and unwavering faith as I walk the path toward healing, knowing that Your love and healing power surround me, for But for you who fear my name, the sun of righteousness shall rise with healing in its wings. (Malachi 4:2)

Praying For Courage To Overcome Fears And Insecurities

God, I pray for courage to overcome fears and insecurities. Fill me with Your strength and assurance, reminding me that You are with me every step of the way, for Have I not commanded you? Be strong and courageous. Do not be frightened, and do not be dismayed, for the LORD your God is with you wherever you go. (Joshua 1:9)

Gracious Lord, I seek Your help in conquering fears and insecurities. Grant me the confidence to step out of my comfort zone, trusting in Your plans and purposes for my life, for For God gave us a spirit not of fear but of power and love and self-control. (2 Timothy 1:7)

Almighty God, I ask for Your grace to overcome fears and insecurities. Help me to find my identity and worth in You, knowing that I am fearfully and wonderfully made, for So do not fear, for I am with you; do not be dismayed, for I am your God. I will strengthen you and help you; I will uphold you with my righteous right hand. (Isaiah 41:10)

Lord Jesus, I pray for Your intervention in conquering fears and insecurities. Grant me the courage to confront the lies that hold me back, replacing them with Your truth and the assurance of Your unfailing love, for The LORD is my light and my salvation—whom shall I fear? The LORD is the stronghold of my life—of whom shall I be afraid? (Psalm 27:1)

God of all courage, I seek Your help in overcoming fears and insecurities. Empower me to embrace vulnerability, to trust in Your strength, and to let go of self-doubt, for But Jesus immediately said to them: 'Take courage! It is I. Don't be afraid.' (Matthew 14:27)

Praying For Courage To Overcome Fears And Insecurities

Loving Father, I ask for Your grace to navigate fears and insecurities with faith. Teach me to lean on Your promises, to cast my anxieties upon You, and to find solace in Your perfect love that casts out fear, for When I am afraid, I put my trust in you. (Psalm 56:3)

Merciful God, I pray for Your guidance in overcoming fears and insecurities. Grant me the strength to face challenges with confidence, the wisdom to seek support when needed, and the trust to surrender my fears to You, for Be strong and courageous. Do not fear or be in dread of them, for it is the LORD your God who goes with you. He will not leave you or forsake you. (Deuteronomy 31:6)

Lord Jesus, I seek Your help in conquering fears and insecurities. Teach me to trust in Your power and provision, to find my security in You alone, and to step out in faith, knowing that You are my strength and refuge, for I can do all things through him who strengthens me. (Philippians 4:13)

God, I ask for Your wisdom in navigating fears and insecurities. Grant me the discernment to identify the roots of my fears, the courage to face them head-on, and the faith to trust in Your plans and purposes for my life, for For I, the LORD your God, hold your right hand; it is I who say to you, 'Fear not, I am the one who helps you.' (Isaiah 41:13)

Lord Jesus, I pray for Your divine intervention in overcoming fears and insecurities. Fill me with Your peace, strengthen my resolve, and grant me the courage to step into the fullness of who You created me to be, for The LORD is my strength and my shield; my heart trusts in him, and he helps me. (Psalm 28:7)

Seeking Patience And Endurance In Times Of Adversity

God, I pray for patience and endurance in times of adversity. Grant me the strength to persevere, the patience to wait upon Your timing, and the endurance to keep pressing forward, for But those who hope in the LORD will renew their strength. They will soar on wings like eagles; they will run and not grow weary, they will walk and not be faint. (Isaiah 40:31)

Gracious Lord, I seek Your help in cultivating patience and endurance during times of adversity. Teach me to trust in Your faithfulness and to remain steadfast in the face of trials, for The LORD is good to those who wait for him, to the soul who seeks him. (Lamentations 3:25)

Almighty God, I ask for Your grace to endure and remain patient in times of adversity. Fill me with Your peace and remind me that Your plans are greater than any challenge I may face, for And let us not grow weary of doing good, for in due season we will reap, if we do not give up. (Galatians 6:9)

Lord Jesus, I pray for Your intervention in cultivating patience and endurance during times of adversity. Help me to lean on Your strength, to trust in Your sovereignty, and to find comfort in Your promises, for The LORD is my strength and my shield; my heart trusts in him, and he helps me. My heart leaps for joy, and with my song, I praise him. (Psalm 28:7)

God of all comfort, I seek Your help in finding patience and endurance in times of adversity. Fill me with Your peace that surpasses all understanding and grant me the perseverance to endure, for Count it all joy, my brothers, when you meet trials of various kinds, for you know that the testing of your faith produces steadfastness. (James 1:2-3)

Seeking Patience And Endurance In Times Of Adversity

Loving Father, I ask for Your grace to navigate times of adversity with patience and endurance. Teach me to trust in Your wisdom, to seek Your guidance, and to find strength in Your presence, for Be strong and courageous. Do not fear or be in dread of them, for it is the LORD your God who goes with you. He will not leave you or forsake you. (Deuteronomy 31:6)

Merciful God, I pray for Your guidance in seeking patience and endurance during times of adversity. Grant me the perspective to see challenges as opportunities for growth, the patience to endure hardships, and the trust to know that You are working all things for my good, for And we know that for those who love God all things work together for good, for those who are called according to his purpose. (Romans 8:28)

Lord Jesus, I seek Your help in cultivating patience and endurance during times of adversity. Teach me to surrender my burdens to You, to find rest in Your presence, and to trust in Your perfect timing, for Come to me, all who labor and are heavy laden, and I will give you rest. (Matthew 11:28)

God, I ask for Your wisdom in nurturing patience and endurance in times of adversity. Help me to remain focused on You, to lean on Your promises, and to find strength in the assurance of Your faithfulness, for I can do all things through him who strengthens me. (Philippians 4:13)

Lord Jesus, I pray for Your divine intervention in seeking patience and endurance during times of adversity. Grant me the grace to trust in Your plans, the perseverance to endure challenges, and the patience to wait upon Your perfect timing, for Wait for the LORD; be strong, and let your heart take courage; wait for the LORD! (Psalm 27:14)

Asking For Wisdom In Seeking Help And Support When Needed

God, I pray for wisdom in seeking help and support when needed. Grant me the discernment to recognize when I need assistance, the humility to reach out, and the wisdom to choose the right people to confide in, for Plans fail for lack of counsel, but with many advisers, they succeed. (Proverbs 15:22)

Gracious Lord, I seek Your help in cultivating wisdom to seek help and support when needed. Teach me to overcome self-reliance and embrace the strength found in vulnerability and community, for Carry each other's burdens, and in this way, you will fulfill the law of Christ. (Galatians 6:2)

Almighty God, I ask for Your grace to guide me in seeking help and support when needed. Help me to recognize that it is not a sign of weakness but a step toward growth and healing, for For where two or three gather in my name, there am I with them. (Matthew 18:20)

Lord Jesus, I pray for Your intervention in seeking wisdom to ask for help and support. Grant me the courage to acknowledge my limitations, the strength to lean on others, and the discernment to choose wise and trustworthy individuals to walk alongside me, for Listen to advice and accept discipline, and at the end, you will be counted among the wise. (Proverbs 19:20)

God of all comfort, I seek Your help in finding wisdom to seek help and support when needed. Fill me with the humility to admit my weaknesses and the wisdom to seek assistance from those who can provide guidance and care, for He heals the brokenhearted and binds up their wounds. (Psalm 147:3)

Asking For Wisdom In Seeking Help And Support When Needed

Loving Father, I ask for Your grace to navigate the path of seeking help and support. Help me to overcome pride, to embrace vulnerability, and to find strength in the community of believers, for And let us consider how to stir up one another to love and good works. (Hebrews 10:24)

Merciful God, I pray for Your guidance in seeking help and support when needed. Grant me the wisdom to recognize the value of seeking counsel, the humility to admit my struggles, and the courage to reach out for assistance, for Do not be wise in your own eyes; fear the LORD and shun evil. (Proverbs 3:7)

Lord Jesus, I seek Your help in cultivating wisdom to seek help and support when needed. Teach me to find strength in unity, to share my burdens with others, and to trust in Your provision through the love and care of those around me, for Bear one another's burdens, and so fulfill the law of Christ. (Galatians 6:2)

God, I ask for Your wisdom in seeking help and support when needed. Grant me the discernment to seek guidance from those who can provide wisdom, compassion, and encouragement, for The wise in heart accept commands, but a chattering fool comes to ruin. (Proverbs 10:8)

Lord Jesus, I pray for Your divine intervention in seeking help and support when needed. Guide me to individuals who can offer wisdom, counsel, and support, and grant me the courage to reach out and embrace the assistance that You provide through them, for Plans are established by seeking advice; so, if you wage war, obtain guidance. (Proverbs 20:18)

Faith And Hope In Overcoming Obstacles

God, I pray for the strength to invoke faith and hope in overcoming obstacles. Help me to trust in Your unfailing love and to have unwavering faith in Your power to overcome all challenges, for Now faith is confidence in what we hope for and assurance about what we do not see. (Hebrews 11:1)

Gracious Lord, I seek Your help in cultivating faith and hope in the face of obstacles. Fill me with the assurance that with You, all things are possible, and grant me the hope that anchors my soul, for For I know the plans I have for you, declares the LORD, plans to prosper you and not to harm you, plans to give you hope and a future. (Jeremiah 29:11)

Almighty God, I ask for Your grace to overcome obstacles by faith and hope. Teach me to fix my eyes on You, to trust in Your promises, and to find comfort in the assurance that You are working all things for my good, for And we know that in all things God works for the good of those who love him, who have been called according to his purpose. (Romans 8:28)

Lord Jesus, I pray for Your intervention in faith and hope in the face of obstacles. Grant me the courage to step out in faith, the perseverance to endure, and the hope that strengthens my resolve, for So do not fear, for I am with you; do not be dismayed, for I am your God. I will strengthen you and help you; I will uphold you with my righteous right hand. (Isaiah 41:10)

God of all hope, I seek Your help in faith and hope to overcome obstacles. Fill me with Your peace that surpasses all understanding, and grant me the unwavering faith to believe that You are working for my good, for May the God of hope fill you with all joy and peace as you trust in him, so that you may overflow with hope by the power of the Holy Spirit. (Romans 15:13)

Faith And Hope In Overcoming Obstacles

Loving Father, I ask for Your grace to navigate obstacles with faith and hope. Teach me to rely on Your strength, to surrender my worries to You, and to trust that Your plans for me are far greater than any challenge I may face, for But seek first his kingdom and his righteousness, and all these things will be given to you as well. (Matthew 6:33)

Merciful God, I pray for Your guidance in faith and hope in the midst of obstacles. Help me to remain steadfast in my belief, to cling to the promises of Your Word, and to find strength in the hope that comes from knowing You, for And my God will meet all your needs according to the riches of his glory in Christ Jesus. (Philippians 4:19)

Lord Jesus, I seek Your help in faith and hope in overcoming obstacles. Teach me to walk by faith and not by sight, to trust in Your guidance, and to find hope in Your resurrection power, for I can do all this through him who gives me strength. (Philippians 4:13)

God, I ask for Your wisdom in cultivating faith and hope in the face of obstacles. Fill me with Your Holy Spirit, renew my mind, and help me to see beyond my circumstances, for Therefore, since we are surrounded by such a great cloud of witnesses, let us throw off everything that hinders and the sin that so easily entangles. And let us run with perseverance the race marked out for us. (Hebrews 12:1)

Lord Jesus, I pray for Your divine intervention in faith and hope to overcome obstacles. Grant me unwavering faith to believe in Your promises, unshakeable hope to persevere through challenges, and the confidence to know that You are with me every step of the way, for Trust in the LORD with all your heart and lean not on your own understanding. (Proverbs 3:5)

SECTION 7

PRAYERS FOR GROWTH AND GRATITUDE

Praying For The Ability To Learn And Grow From Setbacks

God, I pray for the ability to learn and grow from setbacks. Grant me the humility to embrace failure as an opportunity for growth, the wisdom to reflect on my experiences, and the perseverance to rise above challenges, for The righteous falls seven times and rises again. (Proverbs 24:16)

Gracious Lord, I seek Your help in cultivating a teachable spirit to learn and grow from setbacks. Guide me to find valuable lessons in every setback, to seek Your guidance in making necessary adjustments, and to move forward with resilience, for Consider it pure joy, my brothers and sisters, whenever you face trials of many kinds, because you know that the testing of your faith produces perseverance. (James 1:2-3)

Almighty God, I ask for Your grace to overcome setbacks and embrace growth. Help me to trust in Your purpose even when facing obstacles, to find strength in Your promises, and to seek Your guidance in learning from setbacks, for For I know the plans I have for you, declares the LORD, plans to prosper you and not to harm you, plans to give you hope and a future. (Jeremiah 29:11)

Lord Jesus, I pray for Your intervention in learning and growing from setbacks. Grant me the courage to face my failures, the wisdom to seek understanding, and the faith to trust in Your redemptive power, for And we know that in all things God works for the good of those who love him, who have been called according to his purpose. (Romans 8:28)

God of all wisdom, I seek Your help in learning and growing from setbacks. Grant me the discernment to see setbacks as opportunities for growth, the patience to persevere through challenges, and the faith to trust in Your guidance, for Trust in the LORD with all your heart, and do not lean on your own understanding. (Proverbs 3:5)

Praying For The Ability To Learn And Grow From Setbacks

Loving Father, I ask for Your grace to navigate setbacks with a growth mindset. Teach me to find resilience in the face of failure, to learn from my mistakes, and to trust in Your process of refining and shaping me, for I press on toward the goal to win the prize for which God has called me heavenward in Christ Jesus. (Philippians 3:14)

Merciful God, I pray for Your guidance in learning and growing from setbacks. Grant me the humility to seek feedback and guidance, the perseverance to keep trying, and the wisdom to make necessary adjustments, for Do not be afraid; do not be discouraged, for the LORD your God will be with you wherever you go. (Joshua 1:9)

Lord Jesus, I seek Your help in learning and growing from setbacks. Teach me to surrender my disappointments to You, to trust in Your plan for my life, and to find strength in Your grace to move forward with resilience and wisdom, for And he said to me, 'My grace is sufficient for you, for my power is made perfect in weakness.' (2 Corinthians 12:9)

God, I ask for Your wisdom in navigating setbacks and embracing growth. Help me to persevere with a hopeful spirit, to learn from my experiences, and to trust in Your ability to turn setbacks into stepping stones toward greater things, for We are hard-pressed on every side, but not crushed; perplexed, but not in despair. (2 Corinthians 4:8)

Lord Jesus, I pray for Your divine intervention in learning and growing from setbacks. Grant me the strength to rise above failures, the humility to seek Your guidance, and the wisdom to apply the lessons learned, for For the Spirit God gave us does not make us timid, but gives us power, love, and self-discipline. (2 Timothy 1:7)

Seeking Gratitude And Humility In Academic Accomplishments

God, I pray for the ability to seek gratitude and humility in my academic accomplishments. Help me to recognize that all knowledge and achievements come from You, and to approach them with a humble heart, for But by the grace of God I am what I am, and his grace to me was not without effect. (1 Corinthians 15:10)

Gracious Lord, I seek Your help in cultivating gratitude and humility in my academic accomplishments. Teach me to acknowledge the contributions of others, to be thankful for the opportunities I've been given, and to use my knowledge and skills to serve and uplift others, for Let the one who boasts boast in the Lord. (1 Corinthians 1:31)

God, I ask for Your grace to overcome pride and embrace gratitude in my academic accomplishments. Help me to celebrate the achievements of others, to recognize the support I've received, and to approach success with a heart full of gratitude, for Every good and perfect gift is from above, coming down from the Father of the heavenly lights, who does not change like shifting shadows. (James 1:17)

Lord I pray for Your intervention in seeking gratitude and humility in my academic accomplishments. Grant me the wisdom to use my knowledge and talents for the betterment of society, the humility to acknowledge my limitations, for What do you have that you did not receive? And if you did receive it, why do you boast as though you did not? (1 Corinthians 4:7)

Seeking Gratitude And Humility In Academic Accomplishments

Loving Father, I ask for Your grace to navigate academic accomplishments with gratitude and humility. Help me to approach success as a gift from You, to honor those who have contributed to my growth, and to remain humble in the face of achievements, for The fear of the LORD is the beginning of wisdom, and knowledge of the Holy One is understanding. (Proverbs 9:10)

Merciful God, I pray for Your guidance in seeking gratitude and humility in my academic accomplishments. Grant me the discernment to recognize that true success lies in using my knowledge to make a positive impact in the lives of others, for Do nothing out of selfish ambition or vain conceit. Rather, in humility value others above yourselves. (Philippians 2:3)

Lord Jesus, I seek Your help in cultivating gratitude and humility in my academic accomplishments. Teach me to view my achievements as opportunities to glorify You, to express gratitude for the support and guidance I've received, and to remain humble in the recognition that I am a lifelong learner, for Humble yourselves before the Lord, and he will lift you up. (James 4:10)

God, I ask for Your wisdom in nurturing gratitude and humility in my academic accomplishments. Help me to use my achievements as a platform to inspire and encourage others, to acknowledge the contributions of my teachers and mentors, and to give glory to You for the knowledge and abilities You have entrusted to me, for Let everything that has breath praise the LORD. Praise the LORD. (Psalm 150:6)

Seeking Gratitude And Humility In Academic Accomplishments

Lord Jesus, I pray for Your divine intervention in seeking gratitude and humility in my academic accomplishments. Grant me a grateful heart that recognizes the blessings and opportunities I've been given, and a humble spirit that acknowledges that true wisdom and understanding come from You alone, for The fear of the LORD is the beginning of wisdom, and knowledge of the Holy One is understanding. (Proverbs 9:10)

God of all wisdom, I seek Your help in cultivating gratitude and humility in my academic accomplishments. Teach me to see the privilege of education, to be grateful for the opportunities to learn, and to use my knowledge for the benefit of others, for From everyone who has been given much, much will be demanded; and from the one who has been entrusted with much, much more will be asked. (Luke 12:48)

SECTION 8

Prayers for Career Discernment

Praying For The Ability To Handle Success With Grace

God, I pray for the ability to handle success with grace. Help me to remain humble in the face of accomplishments, to use my successes as opportunities to glorify You, and to remember that true fulfillment comes from serving others, for Humble yourselves before the Lord, and he will lift you up. (James 4:10)

Gracious Lord, I seek Your help in cultivating humility and gratitude in handling success. Teach me to recognize that all achievements are gifts from You, to celebrate the accomplishments of others, and to use my success to uplift and encourage those around me, for Let the one who boasts boast in the Lord. (2 Corinthians 10:17)

Almighty God, I ask for Your grace to overcome pride and embrace grace in handling success. Remind me that success is not a measure of my worth but an opportunity to steward the gifts You've entrusted to me for the greater good, for For everything comes from him and exists by his power and is intended for his glory. All glory to him forever! Amen. (Romans 11:36)

Lord Jesus, I pray for Your intervention in handling success with grace. Grant me the wisdom to use my accomplishments for the benefit of others, the humility to acknowledge the contributions of others in my success, and the grace to remain grounded in Your truth, for Each of you should use whatever gift you have received to serve others, as faithful stewards of God's grace in its various forms. (1 Peter 4:10)

God of all wisdom, I seek Your help in handling success with grace. Teach me to walk in humility, to value relationships over achievements, and to use my influence for the betterment of others and the advancement of Your kingdom, for Do nothing out of selfish ambition or vain conceit. Rather, in humility value others above yourselves. (Philippians 2:3)

Praying For The Ability To Handle Success With Grace

Loving Father, I ask for Your grace to navigate success with grace and humility. Help me to resist the temptations of pride and entitlement, to remain grateful for the opportunities I've been given, and to use my success as a platform to inspire and empower others, for Let your light shine before others, that they may see your good deeds and glorify your Father in heaven. (Matthew 5:16)

Merciful God, I pray for Your guidance in handling success with grace. Grant me the discernment to prioritize what truly matters, the compassion to lift others up, and the grace to recognize that success is a journey and not a destination, for But he gives us more grace. That is why Scripture says: 'God opposes the proud but shows favor to the humble.' (James 4:6)

Lord Jesus, I seek Your help in handling success with grace.
Teach me to find my identity in You, to remain rooted in Your love, and to use my success to shine Your light in the world, for Let us not become conceited, provoking one another, envying one another. (Galatians 5:26)

God, I ask for Your wisdom in navigating success with grace.
Help me to use my achievements as opportunities to bring glory to Your name, to extend kindness and encouragement to others, and to always walk in humility and gratitude, for But seek first his kingdom and his righteousness, and all these things will be given to you as well. (Matthew 6:33)

Lord Jesus, I pray for Your divine intervention in handling success with grace. Grant me the ability to approach success with humility, gratitude, and an open heart, using every triumph as an opportunity to glorify You and to make a positive impact in the lives of others, for So whether you eat or drink or whatever you do, do it all for the glory of God. (1 Corinthians 10:31)

Asking For Divine Favor In Scholarship Applications Or Grants

God, I come before You seeking Your divine favor as I embark on scholarship applications. Guide me in selecting the right opportunities, grant me clarity in presenting my strengths and aspirations, and open doors for scholarships that align with Your plans for my future, for Commit to the LORD whatever you do, and he will establish your plans. (Proverbs 16:3)

Gracious Lord, I seek Your help in pursuing scholarships and grants. Bless my efforts as I gather the necessary documents, write essays, and complete applications. May Your favor rest upon me, positioning me for success in securing the financial support needed for my education, for The LORD will open the heavens, the storehouse of his bounty, to send rain on your land in season and to bless all the work of your hands. (Deuteronomy 28:12)

Almighty God, I ask for Your grace to overcome any anxieties and to trust in Your divine favor throughout the scholarship application process. Help me to submit applications that reflect my true potential, to stand out among other applicants, and to receive favor in the eyes of the selection committees, for But seek first his kingdom and his righteousness, and all these things will be given to you as well. (Matthew 6:33)

Lord Jesus, I pray for Your intervention in my scholarship applications. Grant me wisdom in choosing the right opportunities, favor in the eyes of the decision-makers, and peace in knowing that Your plans for my future are secure, for For I know the plans I have for you, declares the LORD, plans to prosper you and not to harm you, plans to give you hope and a future. (Jeremiah 29:11)

Asking For Divine Favor In Scholarship Applications Or Grants

God of provision, I seek Your help in securing scholarships and grants. Guide me in highlighting my unique qualities, experiences, and passions in my applications. May Your favor shine upon me, aligning me with the opportunities that will support my educational journey, for And my God will meet all your needs according to the riches of his glory in Christ Jesus. (Philippians 4:19)

Loving Father, I ask for Your grace to navigate the scholarship application process. Help me to trust in Your divine favor rather than relying solely on my own abilities. Grant me the confidence to present myself authentically and the assurance that Your perfect plan for my future will unfold, for But he said to me, 'My grace is sufficient for you, for my power is made perfect in weakness.' (2 Corinthians 12:9)

Merciful God, I pray for Your guidance in pursuing scholarships and grants. Grant me favor in the eyes of those who review my applications, that they may recognize my dedication, potential, and alignment with their values. May Your favor open doors of opportunity for financial assistance, for The LORD makes firm the steps of the one who delights in him. (Psalm 37:23)

Lord Jesus, I seek Your help in navigating the scholarship application process. Grant me clarity of mind as I articulate my aspirations and goals. May Your favor rest upon me, guiding me to scholarships that will support my educational journey and enable me to make a positive impact in the world, for And whatever you do, whether in word or deed, do it all in the name of the Lord Jesus, giving thanks to God the Father through him. (Colossians 3:17)

Asking For Divine Favor In Scholarship Applications Or Grants

God, I ask for Your wisdom in pursuing scholarships and grants. Grant me favor in the eyes of those who review my applications, that they may see my potential, determination, and commitment to academic excellence. May Your favor pave the way for financial provision and open doors for my future success, for The LORD gives strength to his people; the LORD blesses his people with peace. (Psalm 29:11)

Lord Jesus, I pray for Your divine intervention in my scholarship applications. May Your favor shine upon me as I seek financial support for my education. Guide me to opportunities that align with Your purpose for my life, and grant me the peace and confidence to trust in Your provision and timing, for But let all who take refuge in you be glad; let them ever sing for joy. Spread your protection over them, that those who love your name may rejoice in you. (Psalm 5:11)

Praying For Clarity In Choosing A Career Path

God of all wisdom, I seek Your help in discerning the right career path. Fill my heart with peace and clarity as I explore different possibilities. Help me to listen to Your gentle whispers and to trust Your guidance, knowing that You have a perfect plan for my life, for The LORD makes firm the steps of the one who delights in him. (Psalm 37:23)

Loving Father, I ask for Your grace to navigate the process of choosing a career path. Grant me patience and discernment as I seek Your guidance. May I be open to new opportunities, willing to step outside my comfort zone, and surrendered to Your will for my life, for I will instruct you and teach you in the way you should go; I will counsel you with my loving eye on you. (Psalm 32:8)

Praying For Clarity In Choosing A Career Path

God, I come before You seeking clarity in choosing a career path. Guide me to align my passions, talents, and purpose with the work that will bring fulfillment and make a positive impact. Grant me wisdom to discern Your calling and the courage to step into the path You have prepared for me, for Trust in the LORD with all your heart and lean not on your own understanding. (Proverbs 3:5)

Gracious Lord, I seek Your help in discerning the right career path. Open my eyes to the opportunities that align with Your will for my life. Give me clarity in understanding my strengths and interests, and lead me towards a career that allows me to serve others and bring glory to Your name, for Commit to the LORD whatever you do, and he will establish your plans. (Proverbs 16:3)

Almighty God, I ask for Your grace to overcome confusion and seek clarity in choosing a career path. Illuminate my path with Your wisdom and insight, revealing the gifts and passions You have placed within me. Help me to make choices that align with Your purpose for my life and contribute to the greater good, for For we are God's handiwork, created in Christ Jesus to do good works, which God prepared in advance for us to do. (Ephesians 2:10)

Lord Jesus, I pray for Your intervention in choosing a career path. Grant me discernment to see beyond worldly success and to prioritize fulfilling Your purpose for my life. Guide me towards a career that aligns with my values, ignites my passion, and allows me to make a meaningful difference in the lives of others, for Delight yourself in the LORD, and he will give you the desires of your heart. (Psalm 37:4)

Praying For Clarity In Choosing A Career Path

Merciful God, I pray for Your guidance in choosing a career path. Grant me clarity in understanding my purpose and the courage to follow the path You have laid before me. Help me to trust in Your plan, knowing that You will equip me with the skills and resources needed to fulfill my calling, for For the LORD gives wisdom; from his mouth come knowledge and understanding. (Proverbs 2:6)

Lord Jesus, I seek Your help in discerning the right career path. Open my heart to Your guidance and direction. Grant me clarity in understanding my unique gifts and how I can use them to serve others. May my career choices align with Your purpose and bring glory to Your name, for But seek first his kingdom and his righteousness, and all these things will be given to you as well. (Matthew 6:33)

God, I ask for Your wisdom in choosing a career path. Help me to surrender my plans and desires to You, and to seek Your will above all else. Grant me clarity in recognizing the path that aligns with my purpose and brings fulfillment, knowing that You are the ultimate source of guidance and direction, for The heart of man plans his way, but the LORD establishes his steps. (Proverbs 16:9)

Lord Jesus, I pray for Your divine intervention in choosing a career path. Grant me the patience to wait for Your perfect timing and the courage to step into the unknown with trust. May I find clarity through prayer, reflection, and seeking wise counsel, knowing that You will lead me on the path that aligns with Your divine plan, for Your word is a lamp for my feet, a light on my path. (Psalm 119:105)

About the Author

Eddie James is an internationally renowned worship artist who has ministered with many of the world's most impactful ministries: Bishop T.D. Jakes, Lou Engle, Bill Johnson, Perry Stone, Karen Wheaton, and Kirk Franklin, to name a few. He is the Associate Pastor and Worship and Arts Director for Nations Church - Daniel Kolenda, Pastor.

His music has climbed to the top of the Billboard Charts because of his songwriting, production, and artistry. His works have been featured on Fox News, Glen Beck, Oprah Winfrey Network, and "Lion of Judah," produced by Warner Brothers. His music and sound are sought after around the world, evident by his appearances on TBN, God-TV, Daystar, "It's Supernatural" – Sid Roth, and Charisma Magazine." Eddie's music is the sound that trumpets his heart for both God and the broken.

Eddie rescues, restores, and disciples youth who are coming out of drug addiction, street life, gangs, violence, abuse, and perverse lifestyles through his recovery program called Dream Life and Discipleship 'N Arts (DNA) programs. These highly effective programs have empowered youth to experience a life of freedom and discover their true significance. Because of this DNA, Eddie James Ministries and Dream Life have helped hundreds of youth experience a life of freedom and discover their true significance – many of whom now have ministries of their own, or are serving in powerful ministries and churches. Eddie James is clearly a voice anointed to SHIFT a generation back to the heart of God.

Book Titles

Prayer Points for Women
Prayer Points for Pregnancy
Prayer Points for Finding a Mate
Prayer Points for Marriage
Prayer Points for Parenting
Prayer Points for Teenagers
Prayer Points for Students
Prayer Points for your Husband
Prayer Points for your Wife
Prayer Points for Inner Healing for Women
Prayer Points for Inner Healing for Men
Prayer Points for Mental Healing
Prayer Points for Self Confidence
Prayers for Self Image
Prayer Points for Career
Prayer Points for Forgiveness
Prayer Points for Grief Recovery
Prayer Points for Drug Recovery
Prayer Points for Moral Freedom
Prayer Points for Overcoming Stress and Depression
Prayer Points for Deliverance
Prayer Points for Overcoming Fear and Worry
Prayer Points for Healing
Prayer Points for Purpose and Destiny
Prayer Points for Success

BOOK TITLES

Prayer Points for Reaching your Potential
Prayer Points for Business
Prayer Points for Financial Freedom
Prayer Points for Life's Decision
Prayer Points for Spritual Warfare
Prayer Points for Protection
Prayer Points for Praying for your City
Prayer Points for Praying for your Nation
Prayer Points for Pastors
Prayer Points for Leadership
Prayer Points for Financial Prosperity
Prayers for Self Image
Prayer Points for Forgiveness
Prayer Points for Spiritual Warfare

We want to hear from You.

If this book has impacted or inspired you in any way, please share your story with us. Your testimony has the power to encourage others in their spiritual journey.

Whether a particular passage spoke to your heart, a prayer connected with you deeply, or you felt closer to God through quiet reflection as you read, we would love to hear how this book blessed you.

Please take a few minutes to write out your testimony and email it to **testimony@pneumalife.com** or visit our website at www.pneumalife.com/testimony to share your experience.

Your story matters - it helps spread the transformative message of God's love and grace. Thank you for partnering with us on this journey of faith. May you continue to feel God's presence guiding your path today and always.

With gratitude,
Pneuma Life Publishing

www.ingramcontent.com/pod-product-compliance
Lightning Source LLC
LaVergne TN
LVHW050600061026
849616LV00031B/364